ISBN 978-0-364-00055-7
PIBN 10801527

Educational Maxims of Dr. Maeser

Dr. Maeser was a strong advocate of the idea that the school and the home should work in unison, stand side by side in the responsible task of educating the child:

"Let your first 'good morning' be to your Father in heaven."

"Character, so to speak, is the timber that man is made of. The fireside, the mother's knee, the father's example, should be the proper starting point-for such a training."

"No mother lets her infant crawl or walk any farther than she can control its movements, to preserve it from the possibility of accident. This illustrates the principle to be kept in view when the consideration of character is concerned."

"It is the fashion in Chinese gardening to force trees and shrubs out of their natural way of growing into all kinds of fantastic shapes, according to the fancy and notion of their master. There is a great deal of Chinese gardening going on in education."

"In the family circle parental authority, and filial love and respect should be sufficient safeguards against any improprieties. Figuratively speaking, the length of the rope of discretionary action should be measured out to children in proportion to their moral, intellectual and spiritual capacities."

"In religious as well as in all kinds of public assemblies, even in theatres and places of amusement, children are to be taught the principle of respect and reverence for the place, the occasion, the property and for the feelings of others. This principle is urged upon the parents for cultivation at their firesides."

"All education commences in the family circle, for father and mother are to the child the first object lesson on which to practice the glorious principle of reverence. There is no people among whom the principle of reverence is less cultivated than it is among the Americans, and it is traceable directly to the sins of omission at the firesides of the nation."

"The strongest incentives to the faithful performances of any duty are, comprehension of its rightfulness, honor, mutual confidence and the cultivation of the proper use, of free agency. Compulsion may enforce compliance with some requirements, but will never convey conviction of its rightfulness in the mind of a pupil or child. If conviction comes at all, it must come by other means. Corporal or physical punishment of any kind is illogical, and is not a natural sequence or result of the offense, but must of necessity bear to some extent the character of arbitrariness."

Dr. Karl Gottfried Maeser

Born January 16, 1828, Meissen, Germany; died Salt Lake City, Utah, February 16, 1901

"It has been my custom, to place my students upon their word of honor when entering the Academy. A young man once asked me what the word, 'honor,' meant. I answered him, 'If I should give you my word of honor about anything, I would die before I would break it.' He asked me no further questions on the subject."

IMPROVEMENT ERA

Vol. XXX   FEBRUARY, 1927   No. 4

MEMORY OF KARL G. MAESER HONORED

Story Told of his Tact with Boys and his Love for Them

A quarter of a century and a year will have passed this 16th of February since the death of the beloved teacher, Karl Gottfried Maeser, the founder, under President Brigham Young, of the Brigham Young University at Provo. He was born over ninety-nine years ago at Meissen, Saxony, Germany, in the little old house still standing and known as No. 10. Zscheilaer Strasse. The old place is now owned and inhabited by the family of Robert Bernock, a shoemaker by trade.

On November 19, 1926, a large number of Church officers and members, including one apostle, six conference presidents, and seventy-seven missionaries, together with official representatives of American and German interests, and citizens of Saxony, gathered at Meissen to do honor to the memory of Dr. Karl G. Maeser, and to unveil a memorial plate, which had been placed upon the outer wall of the house, facing the street. Hon. George P. Waller, U. S. Consul, Dresden, and Vice-Consul Duran Grinstead, represented America at the services. Representatives of the schools and of the Burgomeister of Meissen were also in attendance. The plan had been previously suggested by Dr. James E. Talmage, president of the European mission, who, with others, had visited the home, viewed the room in which Brother Maeser was born, and obtained a willing consent of the present owner, of the premises for the purposes undertaken.

The tablet was unveiled by Myron Maeser Crandall, a grandson of Dr. Maeser, who is now a missionary in Germany. It is an oblong stone, 39½ x 31½ inches, and the text of the inscription, written by Dr. Talmage, and translated into German, is inscribed with deep-cut letters into the "massive plate of enduring diabase," as follows:

Entered at the Post Office, Salt Lake City, Utah, as second class matter. Acceptance for mailing at special rate of postage provided for in Section 1103, Act of October 3, 1917, authorized on July 2, 1918, $2 per annum.
Address Room 406, Church Office Building, Salt Lake City, Utah.

Top: President Talmage delivering the memorial address
Bottom: View of the building and the people during the delivery of the address

"IN THIS HOUSE, ON JANUARY 16, 1828, WAS BORN KARL GOTT-FRIED MAESER. * * * NEXT TO HIS GOD HE LOVED HIS FELLOW-MEN, AND TO THEIR BETTERMENT DEVOTED HIS LIFE. * * * TO KNOW HIM WAS TO BE WELL TAUGHT. * * * HE WAS AN EMINENT EDUCATOR, A PROFOUND THEOLOGIAN AND AN EXEMPLAR OF TRUE RELIGION. * * * IN THE CHURCH OF JESUS CHRIST OF LATTER-DAY SAINTS, TO-WHICH HE DEVOTED THE FULL POWERS OF HIS SPLENDID MANHOOD, HE WAS ONE OF THE LORD'S LEADERS. * * * HE DIED IN HONOR ON FEBRUARY 16, 1901, AT SALT LAKE CITY, UTAH, UNITED STATES, AMERICA."

The memorial address, an eloquent tribute, was given by President James E. Talmage, written in English, translated into German, and read in German by the speaker. The prayer of dedication followed the address; and while President Talmage offered the prayer the great assembly stood with heads bowed and with every manifestation of reverential attention.

Retiring President Fred Tadjë conducted the services at the house, and, in the course of his remarks, following the dedication, illustrated what prayer and patience can do, and called attention to the practical results that really count in the service of God and humanity, and in the redemption of the wayward.

In the course of his remarks, President Tadje retold the following story, translated from the German for the *Millennial Star*, December 9, which number is largely devoted to the proceedings. The story applies to teachers and parents in the government and redemption of obstinate boys today, as it did in the days of Dr. Maeser, the great Church teacher:

In the southern part of Utah there lived a poor widow and her son, the latter a wild, impudent, intractable youth, whose transgressions often brought his mother into sore distress. He was known as the terror of the town. He had almost reached the period of manhood without having curbed this insubordination. One evening the bishopric of the ward in which he lived proposed to him that he attend the Brigham Young Academy. In this proposition they had two purposes; one was that they might rid themselves of him, and the other that he might improve himself. They were willing to furnish the money if he would but go.

When this proposition was placed before him he accepted; his mother agreed to it; and in a very short time he was enrolled as a student in the above mentioned school. One glance was sufficient to convince his associates that he was not to be trifled with. He came to school with his books under his arm and a six-shooter in his hip pocket. It was difficult for him to accustom himself to his new surroundings; he felt like a young bronco, newly saddled.

Before the end of the first week he had a difficulty with his teacher, to whom he manifested such a degree of insubordination that his instructors appealed to President Maeser of the Academy to have him suspended. With bowed head the Principal listened, without uttering a word. Finally he broke the silence and said, "Try him once more; he is the son of a widow whose entire hope is centered in him. She knows her boy better than we do. She hopes and prays that some day he will see the foolishness of his ways and change them. She has written me several letters in which she has pleaded with me to try and save him. I have promised that I would do my best, and I will keep my promise. Give him one more chance."

The instructors returned to their class-rooms in compliance with the Master's wishes. Try as they would, all their efforts were in vain, and the young man remained wholly uncontrollable. At the end of another week the instructors returned to the office of the Principal and placed two propositions before him. The one was that this young man should be dismissed from the school forthwith; the other, that in the event the Principal could not see his way clear to dismiss him, they would hand in their resignations to take effect immediately. "That young man is a terror," said one of the instructors; "we have done our best, but have failed absolutely." "Send him to me," said Brother Maeser.

In a few minutes the young man entered the Principal's room. "Did you send for me?" he asked in a low but defiant voice.

"Yes, sir," replied the genial Principal. "I sent for your because I have to inform you that you must leave this institution tomorrow morning."

"Good," answered the yet unsubdued youth; he then turned about and left the room.

In the middle of the following night, Brother Maeser awoke from his slumber and thought of the wild youth whom no one seemed able to tame, who was to be expelled from the school on the following morning. He also thought of the anxious widow and how she had pleaded with him that he might save her son. He arose from his bed, knelt by the side of it and laid the matter before the Lord; and this was the purport of his supplication: "Dear Father, there is at this time a young man in our school whom we are unable to control. We have tried to do our best, but, sad to say, we have failed. If there is a way whereby we may reach him, I pray thee in our Redeemer's name to make it known unto us; and thy name shall have the praise, the honor, and the glory."

"I received no satisfaction from my supplication," said Doctor Maeser; "and therefore thought it possible that the Lord Himself had given him up."

The next morning, about ten o'clock, as the Principal was sitting in his office, there came a knock at the door. Following his call, "Come in," the "black sheep" of the flock entered the room.

"Well," said the Principal, "what can I do for you?" The young man, with down-cast eyes, replied: "May I speak with you for a few moments, Professor Maeser?"

"Certainly," was the reply.

The young man's lips quivered; and, with trembling voice, he said: "You will not dismiss me, Brother Maeser, will you? Will you not please give me one more chance?" Brother Maeser sprang to his feet, extended his arms toward this once obstinate youth and exclaimed: "Come to my arms, my son, God bless you! I will not give you up; not one chance, but a thousand chances shall we be glad to give you." The master and the student fell into each other's arms and wept.

This was the turning point in the life of this young man. He studied energetically and worked so industriously that upon various occasions the Principal had to caution him against over-exertion.

You ask, "Whatever became of the boy?" The last we heard of him he was a counselor to the bishop who had sent him to Provo to school partly that the ward might be relieved of his presence. He and thousands of others living today bless the name of Karl G. Maeser, and hold it in honorable remembrance.

The further program on the notable occasion consisted of an address by President Hugh J. Cannon of the Swiss-German mission, together with instrumental and vocal selections. The invocation was by Elder Douglas Wood, and the benediction by the new President of the German-Austrian mission, former Bishop Hyrum W. Valentine of the Third ward, Brigham City, Utah, who arrived in Dresden October 30, and who relieved President Tadje, who had served since April 1, 1923. In addition to the hymns, "O say what is truth?" "O my Father" and "Now let us rejoice," the song, "The teacher's work is done," composed in memory of Dr. Maeser by Annie Pike Greenwood, was sung.

On Dr. Maeser's birthday anniversary in 1908, the faculty and students of the B. Y. U. assembled on Temple Hill, Provo, and dedicated the Maeser Memorial Building, a beautiful monument, to his memory; and an appropriate monument marks the resting place of his body in the cemetery at Salt Lake City. Yet, as Dr. Talmage said; "He needs no material monument to perpetuate his memory. The record of his deeds is inscribed in the hearts of his pupils."—A.

RECENT SCIENTIFIC INVESTIGATIONS
They Substantiate The Book of Mormon

By Alton C. Melville

"The Pompeii of Ancient America," is the title given to the report of A. Hyatt Verrill of the results of the first six months' investigation conducted by him in the interest of the Museum of the American Indian, Heye Foundation, of New York. This expedition of the past year is the first ever conducted in Panama. The reason for the delay in such investigations is the extremely heavy tropical undergrowth. This, along with the tropical weather, have worked havoc with the architectural remains of the American continent, destroying where natural conditions in Greece and Egypt tend to preserve the splendors of the past, according to the investigators.

Nevertheless, remarkable discoveries have been made very recently by scientists. The account given by Mr. Verrill in *World's Work* will be found to be strikingly similar to that given by Moroni and others in the Book of Mormon; the principal difference seems to be only in the author's point of view, the facts are entirely consistent, in both instances. (*World's Work*, January, 1927.)

LOCATION AND SIZE

"And they built a great city by the narrow neck of land, by the place where the sea divides the land.   *   *   *   And the whole face of the land northward was covered with inhabitants." (Ether 10:20).

The locality of Mr. Verrill's investigation is the same, the Panama region. The term "great" in its fullest meaning is very appropriate in describing in size what has already been found, both in area and number of inhabitants. A single temple is being cleared of the heavy tropical growth and excavated at this time by this explorer. It covers, alone, an area of more than one hundred acres; about a tenth of the job is completed. In his report Mr. Verrill says: "My statement that the area supported a vast and teeming population is based on several obvious facts. *First*, the immense number of burials, ceremonial monuments, village sites, and mounds. *Second*, the incredible number of potsherds, stone artifacts, and other manufactured articles scattered over an immense area. *Third*, the enormous size and great number of stone stelai, monuments, etc., which could have been moved and erected only by thousands of hands."

COMMERCE

"And they were exceedingly industrious, and they did buy and sell and traffic one with another, that they might get gain." (Ether 10:22.)

Speaking of former inhabitants of Yucatan, Gregory Mason, who with Prof. Heber J. Spinden of the Peabody Museum of Harvard headed a recent expedition into that vicinity, says, "The bold canals dug by the Mayas for their ships of commerce are filled with heavy reeds and crocodiles.   *   *   *   The Mayas were a nation of traders and farmers whose social fabric rested upon a wide-spread and deep feeling for religion."

INDUSTRIES

"Wherefore, he [Shule] came to the hill Ephraim, and he did molten out of the hill, and made swords out of steel for those whom he had drawn away with him; and after he had armed them with swords he returned to the city Nehor, and gave battle unto his brother Corihor, by which means he obtained the kingdom and restored it unto his father Kib." (Ether 7:9.)

"And they did work in all manner of ore, and they did make gold, and silver, and iron, and brass, and all manner of metals; and they did dig it out of the earth; wherefore, they did cast up mighty heaps of earth to get ore, of gold, and of silver, and of iron, and of copper. And they did work all manner of fine work." (Ether 10:23.)

Quoting Mr. Verrill on this subject: "If, in a country like Egypt, where even flowers are perfectly preserved in burials thousands of years old, only one iron implement has been discovered, what chances of finding iron tools would we have in a tropical land, where burials were in the earth?

"Indeed, less than two years ago, I was scoffed at for suggesting that an entirely new and unknown culture of great antiquity had existed in Panama, but we now have undeniable proofs of the fact.   Moreover, at a depth of five and one-half feet below the surface, at the temple site, among broken pottery and embedded in charcoal, I found a steel or hardened iron implement.   The greater portion is almost completely destroyed by corrosion, but the chisel-shaped end is in good condition.   It is so hard that it is scarcely touched by a file and will scratch glass, and with such an implement it would be a simple matter to cut and carve the hardest stone."

"Oddly enough, no gold or copper objects have been found, although the race was evidently familiar with gold and were experts at working the metal, for a nose-ring of bloodstone beautifully cut and polished is capped at the extremities with wonderfully wrought and fitted gold tips."

CLOTH

"And they did have silks, and fine-twined linen; and they did work all manner of cloth, that they might clothe themselves from their nakedness." (Ether 10:24.)

Although pictures and drawings suggest that these people wore no garments, says Mr. Verrill, yet "the presence of clay spindle weights proves that they used cotton, if not as cloth at least as thread or twine."

TOOLS

"And they did make all manner of tools to till the earth" * * * (Ether 10:25.).

The same explorer has this to say regarding tools: "I am thoroughly convinced that these people, as well as many other pre-historic races, possessed iron or steel tools, and I do not know of a single argument or fact to disprove this. * * * But how can they explain the evidence of tool marks on much of the stone work? Not the irregular indentations which might have been, and very likely were, made by pecking with a stone hammer, but clearly cut, delicate lines and chisel marks. However, we shall leave this for the archae-ological experts to decide. * * * "

ELEPHANTS—DOMESTICATED

"And there were elephants and cureloms and cumoms * * * which were especially 'useful unto man'." (Ether 9:19.)

Although the evidence may be said to be conclusive, that the elephant or mastodon found in the LaBrea tar pits and other places existed at a much earlier time than civilization, yet we have the fol-lowing bit of convincing evidence in substantiation of the Book of Mormon that the elephant has existed since then, and probably was domesticated. Mr. Verrill says, "But perhaps the most interesting and remarkable find of all was a large sculptured stone figure thoroughly elephantine in form and detail. * * * Not only is the body elephantine, but the large leaf-like ears could belong to no other known creature, while the hind knees bend forward, a character peculiar to the elephant. * * * It is difficult to believe that any man un-familiar with the elephant could have conventionalized a tapir or ant bear to the extent of adding broad fan-shaped ears and legs bend-ing forward, while, as a final touch, the creature is represented carrying a load or burden upon its back!"

THE TIME ELEMENT

The Book of Mormon gives us the earliest time of this civiliza-tion as being about 2,000 B. C., or nearly four thousand years ago.

Although Mr. Verrill, in estimating the time, speaks only in very approximate terms, note how he virtually agrees with the sacred record: "At this rate it would require four hundred years to deposit a foot of soil, and an accumulation of ten feet would mean some four thousand years have passed since the first monuments and idols were erected."

*   .*   *   *

And yet someone has said that Joseph Smith wrote the Book of Mormon from his own knowledge. If he did, would it not prove that he was indeed a Prophet and Seer, to possess the knowledge of conditions, the customs of peoples, their occupations and industries, the varieties of animals and the particular time they existed—and this, years before science or any human agency knew?

If, as the fact is, he did not write the book originally, it is true that, as Gregory Mason says, "where a few centuries ago thousands of human beings fashioned a high civilization" they "abandoned their cities to the devouring jungles of the tropics   *   *   *   from causes still wrapt in mystery." Isn't it more reasonable to believe that this record has been brought forth from the earth, as have these other things, only by Divine direction for the spiritual enlightenment of man? The scientific phase is, of course, only incidental.

Bearing on the Book of Mormon

Students of the Book of Mormon are always on the lookout for any item in history or science bearing upon that record, and so the following is submitted:

An account of the tradition among the Chinese, of their first settlement in China, seems to hint at that remarkable migration of the Jaredites from the Tower of Babel to the "great sea which divides the lands," where some of them (doubtless only a part of them) took to the barges which were lighted in so remarkable a manner. Dr. Fisher, of Yale, gives this account:—

"The nucleus of the Chinese nation is thought to have been a band of immigrants, who are supposed by some to have started from the region southeast of the Caspian Sea, and to have crossed the headwaters of the Oxus. They followed the course of the Hoang Ho, or Yellow, river, having entered the country of their adoption from the northwest, and they planted themselves in the present province of Shan-se."

Further to identify these people to the Book of Mormon reader, Dr. Fisher adds, "Although nomads, they had some knowledge of astronomy." Of the occurrences while the migration halted at that point, history, of course, says nothing, but the annual pilgrimage of hundreds of thousands of Chinese to the top of their sacred mount just at the point of the peninsula of Shantung, testifies to the Book of Mormon student very eloquently of the wonderful manifestations received there by the brother of Jared.—*L. A. Wilson*, Manti, Utah.

JOSEPH'S MARRIAGE IN EGYPT

BY E. CECIL MCGAVIN, PRINCIPAL L. D. S. SEMINARY

A question frequently asked of Latter-day Saints, which at first seems difficult to answer, is that concerning Joseph's marriage in Egypt. Africa has long been called the "Dark Continent;" not wholly because so little was known of it, but also because it was the abode of the dark race. Just a few generations after the flood, Egypt had been colonized by the descendants of Ham. The country was discovered by, and named in honor of, Egyptus, the daughter of Ham, who made this land the home of her posterity.

Years later when Northern Africa was rather thickly populated with the children of Ham, Joseph, the Israelite, was sold into Egyptian bondage, where he later gained favor with the ruling class and was received in marriage into their number. It is generally understood that the great majority of the people of Africa were of the black race, maintaining their own dynasties and native rulers. Thus the question is raised as to the validity of the claims of Joseph's two sons, Ephraim and Manasseh, to the 'Royal' blood, and the distinctive position they hold in Israel. If Joseph married an Egyptian princess, whose descendants were denied the Priesthood, how does one justify Ephraim's pretentions to the covenant of the gospel, with its numerous blessings, all of which are denied the children of Ham?

This situation is made even more complex by the following quotations from the Pearl of Great Price:

"Now this king of Egypt was a descendant from the loins of Ham, and was a partaker of the blood of the Canaanites by birth.

"From this descent sprang all the Egyptians, and thus the blood of the Canaanites was preserved in the land. * * *

"Now Pharaoh being of the lineage by which he could not have the right of Priesthood, notwithstanding the Pharaohs would fain claim it from Noah, through Ham. * * *" (Abraham 1:21-27.)

Profane history joins hands with sacred writ in a defense of the claims of Joseph's two sons to the holy Priesthood. Joseph, whose virtue was the cause of his unjust sentence to the horrible prison dungeon, was no person to forget the great promises made to the seed of Jacob, and inter-marry with the children of Ham, thereby making the fulfilment of this remarkable promise impossible.

Joseph was born about the year 1745 B. C. At the age of seventeen he was sold into Egypt, where he remained until his demise, about 1635 B. C., being 110 years old.

Most of the authorities on this period of history are agreed that a race of Semitic people—descendants of Shem, and therefore not

denied the Priesthood—had invaded Egypt, had overthrown the native
rulers and had established their own government. This was the
condition in Egypt at the time Joseph entered as a slave. The ruling
class was not composed of the aborigines. Not all the people living
in Egypt were Egyptians. (See *Improvement Era*, vol. 24, pp. 172-3,
Dec., 1920.)

In this discussion the most famous scholars the world has known,
in this particular field, will be brought upon the stage, introduced to
an inquiring yet interested audience, and be allowed to add the results
of a lifetime of scientific study upon this poorly understood period
of history.

The pioneer in this field was Manetho, an Egyptian priest who
lived in the third century B. C., and who compiled in the Greek
language a chronicle of the Pharaohs. The valuable records of
Manetho were subsequently destroyed, so that most of the statements
from his works are preserved in the writings of Josephus. His story,
in which Josephus concurs, is this:

"In the days of the Egyptian king, Timaeus, the land was suddenly
invaded from the East. The invaders conquered it without a struggle,
destroyed cities and temples, and slew or enslaved the inhabitants. At
length they elected a king who, residing in Memphis, made all Egypt
tributary to him, and established garrisons in all parts, especially eastward,
fearing the Assyrians. The Hyksos dynasty consisted of six kings who
reigned 198 years and ten months. Their whole race was named Hyksos
or 'Shepherd Kings.' When they and their successors had held Egypt for
511 years, the king of Thebes and other parts of Egypt rebelled, and a
long war began. Misphragmuthosis drove the Shepherds from the throne.
They were allowed to depart from Egypt. They went forth with their
whole families and effects, not fewer in number than 240,000, settled in
Judea and built Jerusalem."

The opinions of these two early historians are somewhat modified
by later authorities, but not sufficiently to alter the major conclusions.
Most of the recent scholars have agreed that the Shepherd Kings were
nomadic people of Semitic ancestry, who after leaving Egypt settled
in Palestine.

One thing is certain, these Shepherd Kings were Semitic and
engaged in the pastoral pursuits common to that nationality. Other
things are not so easily ascertained. The date of their conquest is
doubtful. Historians say it was between 2100 B. C. and 1657 B. C.
Breasted insists upon the latter date. West says the Hyksos maintained themselves in Egypt about 400 years, from 2000 B. C. until
1600 B. C. If this last date be true, the return of the native rulers
would have occurred just about two decades following the death
of Joseph.

The very name, Hyksos, is doubtless of Semitic origin. Dr.
Budge, the foremost scholar on the question, says that the word "Hyk"
means king, or prince, while "sos" signifies keepers of flocks or herds.
A name true to the life of the nomadic pastoral Israelites of that day.

The *International Bible Dictionary* defines Aram as the elevated country northeast of Palestine, called in the Greek Mesopotamia. This same word Aram is of Semitic origin also. Shem, the progenitor of the Israelites, had a son named Aram. Abraham's brother, Nahor, had a grandson named Aram. David speaks of Aram-na-ha-raim, which is defined in the above-mentioned dictionary as meaning "Aram, of or between the two rivers."

Dr. Sayce, of similar renown, maintains that, "It was during the domination of one of the three Hyksos dynasties that first Abraham, and later Joseph, must have entered Egypt, and found a ready welcome among a people of kindred race."

It is thought that the invading Shepherds soon adapted themselves to Egyptian manners, leaving the old administration untouched, some of the kings were even assuming Egyptian names. This part of Egyptian history, however, is very obscure. Their monuments, from which most of the knowledge of the period is obtained, are very rare. After their expulsion, the Egyptians who actually hated them, did their utmost to destroy all that reminded them of the despised foreigners. The few remaining statues erected by the Hyksos represent their peculiarities of countenances, and the un-Egyptian arrangement of the beard, and the remarkable head-dress, which distinguishes them from the Egyptians.

Dr. Hales adds materially to our conclusion by his statement that "one of the Hyksos rulers took the Semitic name, Yakeb-bal, meaning, Jacob is God, and another, Yak-eb-baal, meaning Jacob is Lord."

Many of these authorities have concluded that Joseph entered Egypt just at the close of the Hyksos rule. Fausset thinks that Apophis, the last of the Shepherd kings, was the one over Joseph.

Though definite information is lacking on this important period, it is not mere conjecture, in view of the above facts, to suppose that after the Israelites were established in their new home, the Shepherd Kings were expelled from the throne and the native Egyptians restored one of their number to the kingship of their native land, long overrun by foreigners, whose ignoble deeds must now be revenged. This opinion is corroborated by the introductory statement of Exodus:

"Now there arose up a new king over Egypt, which knew not Joseph."

If the dynasty of Shepherds had maintained themselves upon the throne, no new king for generations would have arisen to power "who knew not Joseph." This Israelite who saved all of Egypt from starvation would never have been forgotten or unknown except by the most bitter enemy.

The historical account of Moses continues:

"Behold the people of the children of Israel are mightier than we: Come on let us deal wisely with them, lest they multiply, and it come to pass, that when there falleth out any war, they join also unto our enemies, and fight against us, and so get them up out of the land."

This fact alone would indicate that no bond of tradition, religion or consanguinity united the Israelites and the Egyptians. No common love of country or home institutions was experienced by the two groups. They were diametrically opposed in almost every activity of life, or there would have been no fear on the part of the natives that the Israelites, in time of invasion, would join the enemy. The presence of the Hyksos had taught them a lesson. They must not tolerate any foreign elements in the kingdom that tended towards disintegration.

The outstanding lesson of history is that nothing unites people of common ancestry, religion, tradition and home-land, as will invasion by an enemy state. The approach of an invading foe promotes greater unity than does any kind of internal conditions. Two notable examples will suffice:

During the latter part of the 16th century England was suffering very seriously from internal warfare between Catholic and Protestant. The Spanish king, a faithful supporter of the Pope, thought it a most propitious time to invade England, unite with the Catholic party of Britain and dethrone Elizabeth, thereby reinstating the Papal authority on the Island. Theoretically, it was indeed an appropriate time for the invasion, but as the "Invincible Armada" approached the Chalk cliffs of Britain, the Anglo-Saxon loyalty to home-land proved stronger than allegiance to a foreign ecclesiastic. The spirit of the father-land united every son of Britain. The very elements were stirred by that tension of patriotism, and while united England fought to prevent the landing of that stately Armada, the angry waves dashed scores of the visiting vessels to pieces on the perilous rocks of the North Sea. The English forgot their petty differences of religion, and united in that greater cause of preservation of the home-land. This loss was so disastrous a failure to Spain, the guardian of the sea, that she lost all pride in her navy, and rapidly fell from her exalted position in the maritime world.

This same principle was later illustrated in our own land, when the cancer, Secession, was gnawing at the vitals of the Republic. On April 1, 1861, William H. Seward, Secretary of State, wrote a letter to President Lincoln, requesting that war be declared upon Spain, France and England, in order to bring the seceding states back into the Union, to ally in bonds of friendship and brotherly love to defend the local institutions against the aggression of the most powerful nations of the world.

The great statesman realized that nothing could bring the prodigal states of the South upon their knees before their brothers of the North as an invasion from abroad. Just twelve days after this letter was written, Fort Sumter lay in ruins.

This one argument of Pharaoh's is a strong one in proving the presence of two widely separated nationalities in the same country. There was not a single bond of union between the two, not even that of occupation. Whereas, the previous dynasties of the Shepherd Kings strongly resembled the Israelites in occupation, nationality, and undoubtedly many other activities which tended to unite the two. If there be anything in common among the citizenry of a nation invasion will strengthen these bonds, not break them, as the Egyptians suspicioned.

Egypt's children of the dark skin had an intense aversion for shepherds. Joseph warned his brothers, upon their arrival in the land of the Nile, that every shepherd was an abomination unto the Egyptians. The one class of people excluded from Egyptian temples was the swineherd—the most despicable creature in the Dark Continent. The mistreatment which the Israelites later received was an expression of the dislike the natives harbored for the foreign shepherds; yet, it must be noted that no aversion was shown until after the death of Joseph when a "new king arose which knew not Joseph."

When the Ishmaelites presented Joseph for sale, he was purchased by Potiphar, a high official in the government, and captain of the royal guard. "And Joseph found grace in his sight, and he served him, and he made him overseer of his house, and all that he had he put into his hands." When he was later imprisoned, he was granted similar honors even among the denizens of that miserable abode in squalor and abuse. "And the keeper of the prison committed to Joseph's hands all the prisoners that were in the prison; and whatsoever they did there he was the doer of it."

This was a strange way indeed to treat a despicable shepherd accused of defiling the wife of a royal officer, having legions of soldiers at his command, when the common punishment for such an offense among their own people was death. Potiphar did not suspicion him; his imprisonment was simply to allay the anger of his wife. All this kind of treatment would not have been extended to him by the children of Ham, in spite of the presence of the Spirit of the Lord with him.

Of a later event we read, "And Pharaoh said unto Joseph * * thou shalt be over my house, and according unto thy word shall all my people be ruled."

Joseph was permitted to marry into the royal family, being given Asenath, the daughter of Potipherah, the prince or priest of the city of On. (Gen. 41:46, 50; 46:20.) This was a city of no mean importance, therefore requiring a person of talent and influence to occupy such a position. Thus his marriage was contracted in the very highest circle of royalty. Had the same feeling existed, as was later manifest when the king arose who knew not Joseph, there would have been no conjugal ties.

Pharaoh was very anxious for Joseph's relatives to make their home in Egypt. At no time did he manifest any dislike for the shepherds. In fact the king himself was the owner of "the cattle on a thousand hills," and requested that Joseph select some of his kinsmen "and make them rulers over my cattle." Hence, it is evident that the attitude the rulers possessed respecting shepherds, differed greatly from the Egyptian's idea of the same vocation.

In the presence of these facts, one cannot deny that Joseph's conjugal lot was cast among a kindred race, with common traditions, ideals and ancestry.

The Latter-day Saints can point with pride to their progenitor, whose marriage in Egypt did not annul the great promises made concerning Abraham's seed.

Beaver, Utah.

To A Lost Friend

In days gone by, a friend I had,
A noble, clear-eyed, smiling lad,
Who shared my fortune—good or bad—
    And dwelt within my heart,
Till every brave adventure dared,
Each deed or thought that wasn't shared,
Was robbed of beauty, stripped and bared,
    If he was not a part.

I lost my friend—had he but died,
And I could kneel his grave beside,
Strew it with flowers at even-tide.
    Some comfort it might give;
But even this is not to be,
My tears are shed where none can see;
He lives, but yet is dead to me—
    'Twas friendship ceased to live.

Had he but gone to foreign lands,
To seek, on far-off ocean strands,
Wealth, love, adventure, Fame's commands,
    Then I should never grieve;
But no, I see him every day,
We meet as strangers, grave or gay;
'Twas just his friendship went away.
    While mine can never leave.

At night, when by my bed I kneel,
I ask God's mercy, woe or weal,
That with my friend he'll gently deal.
    And choicest blessings send;
But for myself, I only plead,
Not gold, nor years, nor fame I need—
To this alone, Father, give heed—
    God give me back my friend.

Durango, Colorado   MINERVA PINKERTON TROY

FROM MARTIN LUTHER TO JOSEPH SMITH

BY L. VALESS DEWEY, M. A.

It seems that in God's economy all truly great events are heralded by a period of preparation. Sometimes these periods are of short duration, as in the case of the heralding of the Messiah by John the Baptist. At other times, longer periods of preparation seem to be necessary. The Dispensation of the Fulness of Times, or more particularly the restoration of the gospel in these latter times, seems to have required a very gradual period of heraldry or introduction. For God chooses to work through human agencies. Thus, more than three hundred years passed in the slow, but none the less sure, re-generation of the so-called Christian world from the twilight of the early Reformation to the noon-day of the restoration of the primitive gospel and Church.

The writer desires to point out four steps in the preparation for the restored gospel—a preparation the beginning of which is commonly known to the world at large as the Reformation. That some kind of preparation was absolutely necessary, no thinking person can doubt. And that great leaders should have arisen just at the right time, with just the proper religious thinking to guide the people, is a phenomenon which philosophers try in vain to explain, and for a solution of which only theologians meekly point to the Providence of God. But the leaders came; and the steps were marked:—that the promise of God might be vindicated in the restoring of Christ's gospel in its fulness.

THE FIRST STEP—THE WORK OF MARTIN LUTHER (1517-1546)

Martin Luther was fortunate in having a mother who had taught him from early childhood something of the power of God directly exercised in the lives of men. Hence it was that from the beginning Luther came to think of God as working directly with men and not necessarily only through the Roman Catholic Pope. He, of course, believed in and subscribed to the power of the Pope in his early life. But this adhering to Roman Catholic control was never as blind and as unintelligent, in the case of the future reformer, as was the manner in which most Catholics of Luther's time gave them-selves body and soul to the power and influence of the Church at Rome. It is true that Luther did not at first wish to leave or be excommunicated from the Roman Catholic church. The posting of his ninety-five theses was not an act of militant rebellion. He simply wished the people to know that there was a question in his mind as to whether some of the actions of the Pope and his agents could be justified by scripture and reason. But before the Reformation had advanced very far, the great German reformer gave evidence that he had a very fair working knowledge of what the church needed. Thus we read:

"The Church of Christ requires an honest ministry, diligently and loyally instructed in the Holy Word of God after a pure Christian intelligence, and without the addition of any false traditions.'" (From "Luther's Idea of the Church"—*Luther and the German Reformation*, by Principal T. M. Lindsay, D. D.)

For practical purposes, however, we may distinguish in the work of Martin Luther three very definite contributions, as follow: (1) the freedom of the mind; (2) faith in God; (3) the democracy of the Lord's table. A few words regarding these contributions will be sufficient for the purpose of this article. Without freedom of mind there can be no rational religion. Luther saw this at the beginning of the reformation controversy. The mind *must* be free to think and act for itself. Once free, the mind and soul of the religious follower may seek after God for himself, uninfluenced by the creeds, dogmas, and traditions of men. Hence, faith in God as a direct agency and help may over-ride, if necessary, any interference on the part of popes or other men. Having secured this enjoyment, the individual is now ready, according to Luther, to appreciate and understand something of the sacrifice of Christ for sinful man. He therefore has a right to partake, with individual freedom and purity, of both emblems of the Lord's Supper and be personally strengthened thereby. All this was unusual and even radical thinking for the time in which Martin Luther lived. And the expression of such thinking was punishable by burning at the stake. Yet every well-informed Latter-day Saint will recognize the foregoing contributions as direct stepping stones to a restoration of the full gospel of Jesus Christ.

THE CONTRIBUTION OF JOHN CALVIN (1536-1564)

John Calvin was a very different type of reformer from Martin Luther. Like Luther, he was a great scholar and thinker; but unlike the German reformer, he possessed a legally trained and very logical mind. Luther was a popular hero, with ideas and ideals which appealed to the people in their varied walks of life. Calvin, on the other hand, was exclusive in his highly intellectual life. We think of Calvin as the author of that highly intellectual and wonderfully logical system of predestination philosophy. It is not, however, the intricate working out of this philosophy with which we are concerned in this article. Let the reader, in passing, be reminded of the principle which lay back of the doctrine—a principle which is highly important as a pre-restoration contribution. In brief, Calvin emphasized strongly the direct pre-determining influence of God in the lives of men. It was God, and not the Pope at Rome, who exerted the real and lasting power and influence over the affairs of life, both here and hereafter. This conclusion would take Luther's first contribution a step further.

Not only must the mind be free—free from the Pope, free in itself—but it must also be free in God; that is, it must be free in God's law. So much for Calvin's contribution in theory.

In practice, there was another very important contribution. Luther had been tolerant as a reformer. Not so this leader of the French reformation. Calvin said what he thought; and carried the thought into action, if he could. We read of him:

"Calvin was implacable in his determination to purify the worship of God of all needless adjuncts. All that was calculated to charm and affect the senses was abolished; spiritual worship should be independent of all earthly things, and, should consist of edification by the word, and simple spiritual songs. All the traditional externals that Luther had retained—altars, pictures, ceremonials, and decorations of every kind—were dispensed with." (From *The Period of the Reformation*, by Hausser, p. 249.)

It is not difficult for a Latter-day Saints to see how this change served to assist in the work of the restoration of the gospel nearly three centuries later.

WESLEY TAKES OTHER STEPS TO OPEN THE WAY (1739-1791)

The reader should bear in mind that nearly two centuries went by after the work of Calvin closed before the contribution of John Wesley was given to the world. Many changes had taken place, both in Europe and in the New World. Much had been accomplished in the way of political revolution and development. The masses of the people were, in general, considerably more able to think and act for themselves. Burnings at the stake had ceased. And, save for occasional charges of witchcraft, heresy was not punishable by death, or even imprisonment. In England, a break with the Roman Catholic church had occurred; the Church of England had been formed, and other sects and denominations of various types had arisen and were still arising. England seemed to be, just now, the logical place for further religious awakening. Certainly there was need for such an awakening. For, though the Reformation proper had ended, there was still a crying need for reforming and awakening. And it was here, indeed, that the next outstanding religious reformer arose and made his contribution to the world.

Although the son of a minister of the church in England, John Wesley was not educated and designed for the ministry as was Luther. He was graduated from a college of his own choosing, and was converted to church activity, in the true protestant sense, after he had finished his college course. Accordingly, we may say that Wesley represents, not so much a breaking away from existing churches or orders of religion, as a revival type. That is to say, the great English reformer sponsored and championed a spiritual awakening in religion already generally existing, rather than the founding of a new religion; and this, in spite of the fact that he did become the father, so-called,

of the Methodist movement.   Wesley was a great preacher, a successful
organizer, and an efficient leader.   His theological contribution is tied
up with what he calls the "new birth."   This new birth or regeneration is largely "the working of the Spirit," as Wesley himself puts it.
But there are also intellectual interpretations.   Wesley was inclined to
put repentance first, then faith, after which came baptism or the new
birth.   Regarding baptism, he has this to say:

"Baptism is a sacrament, wherein Christ hath ordained the washing
with water, to be a sign and seal of regeneration by his Spirit."   (*Wesley's
Doctrinal Standards*, by Burwash, p. 453.)

Wesley favored immersion as the correct mode of baptism enjoined
by the New Testament.   He permitted sprinkling, however, and also
allowed and accepted the baptism of infants.   It may be well to add
that Wesley's teaching of baptism by immersion was reinforced by the
Baptist movements, though none of these latter movements produced
an outstanding leader or reformer.

CAMPBELL AS A REMINDER OF OTHER TRUTHS (1812-1866)

It remained for Alexander Campbell to remind the world of
the first three fundamentals of gospel thought, giving their proper
relationships and approximate meanings.   This remarkable leader of
religious thought was of Scotch-Irish descent.   He came to America to
work with his father, who was already a minister of the gospel, in
Pennsylvania.   Young Campbell and his father left the Presbyterian
church because of their mode of baptism.   In 1812 they were immersed
and began to preach for the Baptist church.   Soon, however, Alexander
Campbell disagreed with Baptist doctrine, insisting that faith should
and does come before repentance.   He also taught the Trinity or God-
head as three distinct and definite personalities.   It became necessary,
therefore, to organize a new group or body of religious believers who
became known successively as "Christian-Baptists," "Campbellites,"
and "Christians," or "Disciples."   Campbell contended that his movement was not the founding of a new sect, but a "restoration movement;" i. e., getting back to the primitive church and its practices, by
observing and living the teachings of Christ and the apostles, as they are
found in the New Testament.   Particularly, the contribution of
Alexander Campbell may be summed up in the following extract, taken
from the *New International Encyclopedia*, under the heading, "Disciples
of Christ:"

"The Disciples accept   *   *   *   the tripersonality of the Father,
Son, and Holy Ghost   *   *   *   the divine excellency of Jesus Christ as
the Son of God   *   *   *   the personal mission of the Holy Ghost * * *
the necessity of faith and repentance to salvation   *   *   *   and the importance of baptism and the Lord's Supper as divine ordinances."

Regarding baptism and the Lord's Supper, it may be added that

Campbell taught that baptism was for the remission of sins, and that the Lord's Supper should be observed often—at least once a week. It is especially interesting to Latter-day Saints to know that the followers of Alexander Campbell were quite numerous in the vicinity of Kirtland, Ohio, when the Prophet Joseph Smith established the headquarters of the Restored Church in that place. Also that a considerable percentage of the earthly converts to the Church of Jesus Christ of Latter-day Saints in those days were first followers of Campbell.

A CLOSING PARAGRAPH

Thus was the way opened and the field prepared for the ushering in of the gospel in its fulness. Truly, "God moves in a mysterious way his wonders to perform." The darkness of the middle ages was too pronounced and consuming for a sudden ushering in of the full light of the gospel from heaven. The mind of man was too far removed from truth to comprehend at once the Fulness of Truth. But God, in never-failing wisdom, always prepares the way, working on natural principle and according to natural law. Little by little the seed of reformation was sown. Line and precept were added as they were needed and could be comprehended. Slowly and surely the beliefs of men were moulded by prophets of a minor order. And many reformers and leaders labored in as many lines of activity that the way might be prepared for the Dispensation of the Fulness of Times. In all these activities, political, industrial, and religious revolutions played their part. Not only must the fulness of the gospel be given from heaven and received by a few—it must also be carried abroad with rapidity and accepted gladly, because minds in many climes and nations had been prepared politically, socially, and psychologically to receive it. Hence, let it not be supposed that the theological field alone needed to be ploughed or the doctrinal vineyard pruned. But after all else has been said, the world needed a Luther, a Calvin, a Wesley, and a Campbell. For without their efforts—humanly speaking—the mighty work wrought by Joseph Smith in the restoration of the Restored Church could not have been accomplished.

Tucson, Arizona.

Living

A few simple things I must learn to do,
If I would make my life happy and true:
Work with increasing skill and cheerful will,
Play with merry glee that gives a thrill,
Think with clearness the thoughts that are best,
Pray with fervency and faith of the blest,
Love my neighbor and gladly take his part,
And serve my God with hand, and head, and heart.

NEPHI JENSEN.

AN INDIVIDUAL TESTIMONY OF THE DIVINITY OF JESUS CHRIST

BY MARTHA E. FULLER, OF THE SENIOR GIRLS, PHOENIX, ARIZONA

The sweetest joy that can come to the human heart is the spirit that attends a testimony of the divinity of Jesus, the Redeemer of the world, who is the Light of the world, and by whom and through whom only we can attain unto life eternal. Great men and great women, through all Christian time, have acknowledged this. The poet Tennyson, upon one occasion, while walking through his garden with a friend, was asked this question, "What influence, if any, has Jesus Christ had upon your life?" And the great poet, reaching, plucked a beautiful rose and made this reply, "My friend, all that the sunlight is to this beautiful flower, so is the Spirit of Jesus, the Redeemer of the world, to my life."

We, the young people of the Church, acknowledge this, and look with sorrow and consternation upon the attack now made by the anti-Christ. So far as we are concerned, we stand by the faith of our fathers, and fling back against the gathering clouds of doubt and dissension the faith-destroying argument of the adversary; and today we announce to all the world that, so far as the young manhood and young womanhood of this Church is concerned, God lives, and Jesus is the Christ.

At this time when the divine character and mission of the world's Redeemer are questioned, even by many professing Christians, it is a cause for congratulation and rejoicing that there is still found "faith on the earth"—faith in Jesus Christ as the very Son of God, as the anointed and fore-ordained messenger of Him who "so loved the world that he gave his Only Begotten Son, that whosoever believeth in him should not perish, but have everlasting life."

Among those who hold fast to this conviction, are the Latter-day Saints, or "Mormons." And we announce to all the world that, "We stand for an individual testimony of the divinity of Jesus Christ."

Such a testimony can come but in one way—and that is God's way, not man's. Books cannot give it. Schools cannot bestow it. No human power can impart it. It comes, if it comes at all, as a gift of God, by direct and immediate revelation from on high.

Said Jesus to his chief apostle: "Whom say ye that I am?" Peter answered: "Thou art the Christ, the Son of the living God." Then said Jesus: "Blessed art thou, Simon Barjona; for flesh and blood hath not revealed it unto thee, but my Father which is in heaven."

Such was the basis of Peter's testimony and such is the basis of every real testimony of like character. They all rest upon the same foundation. Testimony means evidence, and a testimony of the gospel may consist of any of its varied fruits; such as: dreams, visions, prophecies, tongues and their interpretation, healings and any other manifestations of the Divine Spirit.

But the greatest and most convincing of all testimonies is the soul's illumination under the kindling and enlightening power of the Holy Ghost—the Comforter, promised by the Savior to his disciples, to abide with them after he had departed, to bring things of the past to their remembrance, and to show them things to come, making manifest the things of God, past, present and future.

By that Spirit, and by that alone, can men know God and Jesus Christ whom he hath sent—to know whom, and to act consistently with that knowledge, is to lay hold upon eternal life. No greater thing can come to men while in the flesh than the knowledge of how to secure that greatest of all heavenly gifts.

To know God, man must know himself, must know whence he came, why he is here, what is expected of him by the One who sent him here, where he is going when he leaves this mortal life, and what awaits him in the great hereafter. The Holy Spirit is the fountain from which flows this knowledge, the most precious that men can possess. By means of it comes the testimony that Jesus Christ was and is divine.

Such a testimony the patriarchs and prophets of old possessed. They were not without the gospel and its glorious gifts. The Holy Ghost did not make its first appearance upon the earth in the days of Jesus and his apostles. Men had seen God before that time, and had enjoyed the sweet influence and wonder-working power of his Spirit. Devised in the heavens before the earth was organized, the gospel had been among men in a series of dispensations, long before it was preached by the apostles in the meridian of time.

"I know that my Redeemer liveth," the cry that came from the depth of Job's sorely tried, suffering, yet patient, soul has been echoed by the hearts of many of the faithful, whose heaven-inspired testimonies have come ringing down the ages, from the days of Adam to the days of Joseph Smith, and the present day. The holy scriptures are filled with testimonies of Christ's divinity, attested by miracles and wonders manifold.

But let us suppose Christ wrought no miracle—suppose he did not walk upon the water, did not heal the sick, cast out devils, give sight to the blind, caused the lame to walk, or did anything that men deem supernatural, was there not that about him which bore unimpeachable testimony to his divinity?

What could be more divine than the life of one who "went about doing good," teaching men to forgive their enemies, to pray for those who persecuted them, and do unto others as they would that others should do unto them? And did he not set the example by asking upon the cross, in the agonies of death, God's pardon upon his guilty murderers? "Father, forgive them, for they know not what they do."

What could be more divine than that? Who but a God could offer such a prayer at such a time? "Greater love hath no man than this, that a man lay down his life for his friends." But there was one who could lay down his life for his enemies, as well as his friends. No mere man could do that. It took a God to die for all men—foes as well as friends—and that act alone stamps divinity upon the character and mission of Jesus Christ.

Phoenix, Arizona.

Yellow Flowers

Yellow flowers are like cheerful people, they brighten odd corners and dingy places. There is something about yellow flowers that radiates cheerfulness like the smile on a friendly face. Yellow flowers carry God's messages to the stricken heart as no other color of flowers can do. Unobtrusively they bloom on wind-swept hills far from the haunts of man, content to make beautiful out-of-way places; they drop their yellow petals, like splashes of sunshine, on the dunes of the gray desert, asking for only the meager dew drops to keep them fresh; they nod in woodland nooks, seen only by birds and bees. They are like the friendly humans who go unconsciously about their silent mission brightening up the community in which they live with the happiness that beams from their faces and the cheerful words that fall from their lips. The dandelion is the humblest of the yellow flowers, it cannot compare with the stately rose, yet little children love it—it is thornless.—*D. C. Retsloff.*

To Measure Success

Out of the failure and out of the fault of you,
  Something rebounds to an ultimate good,
Something that savors the tang and the salt of you,
  Weathers the sinew and gnarl of the wood.

Out of the residue, out of the flaws of you,
  Something is crystalized deep in the dross,
Back of the primitive reason and cause of you,
  Nothing was ever created for loss.

Out of your past there emerges tomorrow,
  Bigger and fuller for tempest and stress,
Out of your failure and out of your sorrow,
  Something is needed to measure success!

Mesa, Arizona.   BERTHA A. KLEINMAN.

TEASING THE DOG

By Ellen L. Jakeman

The richest soil, unsown to better seeds,
Will give its strength to foul and bitter weeds.

Mr. Maxwell was hardly out of sight going toward home, his
big dog, Leone, lumbering at his heels, when Bill Duncan crept
out of the bushes and trees that grew all round this corner of
the Maxwell farm, sheltering orchard and watermelon patch from wind
and frost. Mr. Maxwell had been one of the first men in this locality
to demonstrate, that, by looking out for favorable conditions, fruit
could be grown. This spot, warm, sandy loam, lying fair to the sun,
was ideal, except that it was too far from the house to be watched
constantly. A gang of boys, of which Bill Duncan was the acknowledged leader, had depredated some; and the owner had been neither
slow nor moderate in denouncing the pilfering and the pilferers, and
had made some threats when exasperated that had not bettered matters
to any great extent. His dog, half St. Bernard, and half—no one
knew what,—sometimes stood guard and was a very faithful and obedient animal; slow to learn a new lesson, but it did seem, when once
mastered, some things were learned too well. For instance:—sent one
day to drive a neighbor's cows away from a rather weak place in the
field fence, he went as he was bidden but did not return till next day,
driving the cows many miles out into the hills, because his master
forgot to whistle a retreat to call him back.

Bill Duncan had not been allowed to have a dog of his own; so,
to save his face with the other boys, who nearly all had dogs, he had
rocked, tin-canned and teased all the dogs, saying he hated them. Leone
was one of the dogs he had teased and hectored till he was afraid of
him, and not without cause. Mr. Maxwell had left his son, Tom, on
guard, and had the dog stayed with him, Bill would have kept dis-
creetly out of sight, but he was not afraid of the boy.

The fathers of these two boys were born in the same English
village, worked together in their youth, joined the Church at about
the same time, crossed the ocean in the same ship and traversed the
plains in the same company, and it would seem that nothing could
have disrupted such a friendship; but the conduct of the boys, and
Mr. Maxwell's threats, had brought about a sullen coldness. No more
did they drop in casually to spend an evening, or make it convenient
to walk together to and from their men's meetings or discuss points of
doctrine, agricultural problems or politics.

No; Bill Duncan was not afraid of Tom Maxwell! The melons
were ripe now, and ready for market, delicious to the taste and doubly
desirable because forbidden.

There must be no outcry, so Bill sneaked silently through the grass till with a bound he was on the back of the young watcher:

"You make one yell and I'll paste you one on the jaw. You're a noble watchman, 'Horatio at the Bridge,' to let the Tuscans sneak right up and climb your back without knowing it!" he told his struggling captive. "Come on now, I'm going to put you in the tool house, and sack Rome; otherwise spoken of as eat all the watermelons I want! See?" and he marched the now non-resisting boy, somewhat smaller than himself, to a bin-like shack built against the hill. Tools were kept here for convenience, and recently a sheet-iron camp stove and a small stock of provisions had been added, for it had been necessary to stand guard at the melon patch all night, sometimes. A heavy iron bar fastened the door on the outside, and there were no windows, and when Bill had shoved Tom in, and barred the door, he exulted in the thought that nothing less effective than an ax could open it from the inside.

Bill stayed a few moments to have fun with his captive, but getting no response, turned his attention to the melons.

He had not yet made his selection when he saw Leone, the dog, come bounding back, and realized that he would have to "leg it some" if he got over the fence before he was caught; and he had no curiosity to find out what a dog that had killed several wild animals in fair fight would do to him if he caught him while trespassing.

It was a close shave, but Bill made it to the fence and over. One of the lessons that Leone had learned was to stay hostilities on his own side of the fence, and to make the boys respect the fence line, also.

Safely over, Bill, who felt the dog had cheated him out of a melon, began to taunt and annoy the faithful old guard, who had gone and lain down in front of the tool hut. He had been sent back to stay with Tom, and it was quite possible that he had seen Bill push Tom into the hut as he came through the brush.

Bill flipped small stones to sting the dog, yelped like a coyote, and, what he knew the dog particularly disliked, pointed his finger at him and made a hissing noise.

Leone rumbled deep growls in his throat, and evinced displeasure, but stuck to his post.

Grown tired of this doubtful sport. Bill decided to go elsewhere, and called out to his prisoner: "Hey, Tom! I'd let you out but this hippopotamus you folks call a dog won't let me. So long! I hope you have a pleasant afternoon in the sweat box for being so stingy with your melons.' Getting no reply, Bill walked away whistling. He had not gone far, however, when, chancing to look back, he thought he saw a faint haze of smoke hovering over the rear part of the temporary prison.

"Fire!" he ejaculated—and it is a word to appall the stoutest heart. He watched the haze for a few moments, unable to believe his eyes, and saw the mist of smoke turn to thin spirals. With genuine alarm he rushed back to open the tool-hut door, but making a mental resolve to thump Tom good if he was playing any kind of a trick on him. Bill was on the fence, but the dog, whom he had momentarily forgotten, met him with teeth bared and neck ruff bristling.

The smoke was growing more dense with every minute, and Bill's alarm grew with it. "Oh, Leone, let me come over," he begged. "Tom's in that tool house and it's afire! Can't you understand, you old fool? Tom! Tom!" Bill called, his fright mounting, but there was no answer.

"I've *got* to come over, Leone," he panted; and the quality of terror in his voice gave the dog, through primal instinct, knowledge that something out of the usual was going forward, and he sniffed and whined uneasily; but the abuse, teasing and taunting that had long been his portion from the hands of this boy was one of the lessons he had learned thoroughly.

It is hard to tell, in the changing vicissitudes of life, into whose hands the balance of power will fall, and what terrible reprisal may be taken for an act of oppression, or a ruthless disregard of another's rights. For Bill, this balance of power was invested in the powerful jaws of a dog that he had assiduously taught to hate and fear him. Who could have guessed when he was teasing, insulting and rocking this animal, that the impressions made might become a matter of life and death?

His mind had reasoned swiftly that if he went over in spite of the dog, and he tore him down as he threatened to do, Tom would be no better off; but he could not quit with that obvious conclusion.

"I'll come over right now, if I have to kill you, or you kill me;" said the desperate, white-lipped boy, as he grabbed up the broken limb of a cedar tree that lay near, and again mounted the fence, determined to open the hut door or die in the attempt.

While Bill was getting the club the dog had run frantically around the tool house, even scrambling over the rocks and brush that blocked the back of it, where the fire was making the most headway, and he sent up a long, mournful howl as he turned the corner, that set every nerve in Bill's body quivering with a cold panic.

The fire was gaining, but the dog met Bill at the fence with a murderous growl, that almost seemed as much an accusation as a menace.

Perhaps nothing on earth but the sight of Mr. Maxwell running toward them, gun in hand, would have kept Bill from jumping down into the very jaws of the slavering beast.

Mr. Maxwell whistled, and, obedient as always, the dog turned to his master.

Over the fence went Bill, and in spite of the intense heat, ran to the burning tool house, and whipping off his coat to protect his hands, tried frantically to lift the iron bar that held the door fast, but the heat had warped the wood and he could not move it. All the time he was making these frantic efforts, he was yelling:

"Tom's in here! Tom's in here!" and in his heart he was saying: "Oh, God, perform a miracle and put out this fire. I know you can do anything you wish to! For Tom's sake! For his father's sake! For his mother's sake! Punish me for all I've done but don't let Tom be burned to death for my wickedness."

Mr. Maxwell stared at the shrieking boy, amazed.

"Come away from there, you big fool," he shouted. "You'll be killed!" But the frantic boy did not seem to hear him, as he made prodigious efforts to remove the iron bar from the door.

Then the back part of the roof fell in.

Bill seemed to realize then that all further effort on his part was useless. He walked toward Mr. Maxwell like a feeble old man. He threw away the scorched and smoking coat, and drew his shirt sleeve across his all but blistered face. He came quite close and throwing wide his arms in a gesture of utter despair said to the amazed watermelon grower:

"Shoot me, Mr. Maxwell, shoot me! I'll tell the truth anyhow when I'm arrested, and they will hang me, but I just can't bear a trial, and see how you and Tom's mother will feel, and how my mother and father will feel and everybody will hate me. I know now." As if talking to himself, he continued, "I know now how Cain felt when he killed his brother. Only he *wanted* to kill Abel, and I only meant to tease and bully Tom," and he sank to the earth, a limp and inanimate heap, at the feet of the surprised and puzzled Mr. Maxwell.

Even the dog knew that something was wrong with his arch-enemy. He whined, and nosed the motionless figure.

Tom came out of the brush and followed his father, who had picked the boy up, over the rough furrows to an irrigation ditch.

"I know what's the matter with him, Daddy! He put me in the tool house so he could steal melons, and I thought I would be there till you came back, so I started to build a fire to get me some dinner, and it would not burn very well; and, happening to think of the panel at the back that would not work after the rainy spell, I left the fire and went and tried it. It worked all right, and I forgot about the fire I'd been trying to build and sneaked out through the brush and trees, without letting Bill know. I must have been gone before Leone got back. I wanted you to catch him taking it easy in the melon patch, and give him a good flogging, but I did not think you'd bring a gun when I told you it was just one of our neighbor boys, Daddy!" and there was something in the tone and the sick-sadness of his lad's young eyes that greatly distressed Mr. Maxwell. He was conscious of a poignant desire to rehabilitate himself in the good opinion of his son, but could think of nothing to say.

Having sloshed the face and head of the collapsed boy liberally with tepid water from the irrigation ditch, and not gaining so much as the quiver of an eyelash in response, Mr. Maxwell became alarmed.

"Run for his father, Tom. Go to the field, not to the house

where his mother is. Tell him to come quickly. Poor kid! If he thinks you were burned to death and it was his fault, I can begin to understand why he asked me to shoot him. He was in earnest, too! Well, that is quite a heavy burden of sorrow for a child, poor kid!'' But Mr. Maxwell was talking to his dog, for Tom had sped away at his father's first words, on fleet and almost tireless legs.

Mr. Maxwell was mechanically wetting the boy's face when his father dismounted from a blown plow horse, and came over and took his son in his arms. The limp form seemed to have shrunken in its clothes, and the limbs sprawled every way in obedience to the laws of gravity. He had heard the whole story from Tom who had ridden back, perched like a monkey on the back of the horse. As Mr. Duncan laid the fire-scorched face on his breast, he didn't say a word, but such a groan burst from his lips as set Tom to crying, and Mr. Maxwell to trying to comfort him.

"There was something noble in that boy's soul," old friend, "even if he was mischievous."

That past tense was like a dagger in the heart of Bill's father, who replied: "I've thrashed him for his mischief, and never taken time to find out what was in his soul; but if God will give him back to me and forgive me for being so blind and stupid in the past, I'll surely be a real father to him in the future."

There in that open field, beneath the blue, imperial sky, they sought the great physician, and humbly begged for the life of Bill, the bad boy, suddenly grown so precious. Before they were well through presenting their petition to the Lord, Bill feebly opened his eyes and looked up into his father's face.

"Are you dead, too, Daddy? You know Tom and I are both dead, don't you? I—'' and before his father could answer him, his voice, not much more than a whisper, trailed off into nothingness, and he was again unconscious.

Mr. Duncan arose to his feet with the boy in his arms.

"It will be best for him to wake in his mother's arms, so I'll carry him home. Tom, will you ride the horse over for me?''

Tom caught the grazing horse, and stood at attention.

Mr. Maxwell spread a clean, white handkerchief between Bill's scorched face and his father's rough shirt; and tore down a panel of fence that Mr. Duncan might pass through without jarring his burden. He then picked up his gun and followed along; and with his dog at his heels, and Tom on the horse, they formed quite a startling procession.

Mrs. Duncan saw them coming and, panic stricken, ran to meet them. Seeing the gun in the hands of her neighbor, said, "Oh, Mr. Maxwell, you haven't shot my boy! I know he has annoyed you, and you have made threats, but surely he did not deserve death!''

Knowing what had been in his thoughts when he went to the melon patch, Mr. Maxwell dropped his eyes to his gun, shifted his glance to the dog, and then to his own boy without replying; but her husband hastened to reassure her.

"No, Mary, our good neighbors came to help me home with him. Billy has fainted,—I'll tell you about it later."

They undressed the still unconscious lad, got him into dry clothes, and to bed, and his mother dressed his burns while she listened to the recital of all but tragedy.

Bill was breathing better now, but suddenly he opened his eyes and cried out in anguish: "Tom is in there, Leone! I must go over the fence! Oh, I wish I had never teased you, old fellow!" and he would have scrambled out of bed if kind hands had not restrained him. When fully awake and made to take a look at Tom, alive and safe, he sank back on the bed, and gave way to saving tears.

Mrs. Maxwell was notified and both father and son stayed all night. They kept Tom as exhibit "A" in case Bill should dream the fire over again, which he did so often that they finally put Tom to bed with him, and Bill went to sleep with his hand firmly grasping the collar of Tom's pajamas.

Through that long night those two fathers, who had come near to being enemies over the pranks of their two boys, talked long and earnestly how best to utilize for good the streams of vitality possessed by their children. They did not originate any very startling, or new, ideas, but they remodeled some very good old ones. They decided that during another year the boys should have a melon patch of their own, and they would talk other fathers into the same idea, as a protective measure. The half holidays so desperately desired by all boys should be cheerfully given as a reward for work properly done on other days, and a fishing tackle provided ungrudgingly. And they would take an interest in whatever happened, and give at least a modicum of praise when the boys used good judgment in the various experiences that came to them.

When the Y. M. M. I. A. was organized in their town, and later the Boy Scouts, there were two fathers present who were ready for them, and eager to put their shoulders to the wheel.

And Bill had learned his lesson, in time for it to be a benefit to him, and his sons after him, and the people of the town in which he lived, not omitting dogs and other dumb animals. Not all of us are so fortunate.

Faith

If God had faith in frail, unstable man,
Subject to passions and misleading dreams,
Subject to fears and doubts and idols false,
Subject to vile, satanic beckonings;

Surely we cannot lose our faith in Him,
Him who has stood the test of time and storms,
Him who alone has kept the heaven bright—
Him who has promised us Eternity.

CLAIRE STEWART BOYER.

THE FAITH THAT ENDURED

BY O. B. PETERSON, FORMER PRESIDENT OF THE TAHITIAN
MISSION

"He that endureth to the end shall be saved."—Matthew 10:22.

As the evening shadows cast a dusky mantle over the coral isles
of the South Pacific, a sailing craft of twelve tons put to sea from the
island of Rairoa, Tuamotu archipeligo, bound for Tahiti. Its cargo
was copra; its passengers and crew numbered eleven—five native men,
three native women, a child, a Spaniard and a Chinaman.

The tropic moon smiled pleasantly in lighting their way, and
with the favor of a brisk, steady breeze, the little boat flitted merrily
over the waves, and by morning had landed them safely at the phosphate island, Makatea. They had little to do at this place, and were
soon on their way again to the Eden of the Pacific.

Fortune continued to ride with them for a while, but as the day
waned and the sun sought the horizon, the wind veered to the south
and began vehemently to oppose their progress. Dame Fortune bade
them adieu. They were soon unable to advance farther in the direction desired, so they set their compass for the island of Raiatea, lying to
the west; and thus they continued for the two days following. The
wind, however, steadily increased in velocity until it became a furious
gale; and the sea joined in the game, as if the little craft were a ball to
be tossed to and fro, hither and yon; and not satisfied with mere play,
the angry waves soon began to break over the deck of the boat, in an
effort, apparently, to submerge it entirely. Seeing this, and thinking
probably to thwart the efforts of both ship and sea, the rain beat down
in torrents. The company of unfortunate souls had no refuge from
the fury of Nature's onslaught, but were compelled to remain on deck
and breast the storm, with light or heavy heart as the case might be.
They first reefed their sails, and then finally lowered them altogether,
leaving the frail, little boat entirely to the mercy of the elements; and
further trying to reconcile, rather than oppose, the angry sea, the course
was changed to agree with the running of the waves, which headed
them back for the island of Makatea. The men were ordered also to
put some of the cargo on deck, to afford them all possible protection,
and two anchors were prepared and dropped into the sea at the front
of the ship to help hold it in an upright position. The force of the
wind made it impossible to light the ship's lanterns, so they performed
their necessary tasks and read the compass by the aid of a hand
searchlight.

It seemed to them that matters could not possibly be worse. They
were then approximately fifty miles southwest from Makatea; ominous
night had come upon them; darkness as of the inner recesses of the
earth settled down over the briny deep. They were trying to calm

themselves with the hope that the light of another morning would
bring relief to their anxious hearts. But alas! The action had not
thus been written into their drama; the denouement had been reserved for another time—they had been merely working up to the
climax. At that moment the wind suddenly came in a whirl; the light
craft was caught in its meshes and overturned, and its forlorn occupants
emptied carelessly into the surging billows of the sea. Oh! Could
there be a worse fate? That green, foamy, briny, ghostly, heaving
mass, clutching at them as the arms and suckers of an octopus; and then
to be hurled bodily into its very embrace!

The hero of the occasion was Mohi (Mo-he), a large, well built,
serious-minded native, whom but to know is to admire. His office of
elder in the L. D. S. Church, backed with faith well grounded in the

A SAILING CRAFT OF TWELVE TONS PUT TO SEA

principles and doctrines of that religion, had made him the staying
power among the little company up to this moment of despair. He
had encouraged them; he had told them that morning would bring
a change to their advantage; his advice, his judgment, his faith and
trust in God were held in high esteem by all on board. Among the
passengers of the capsized boat were his son and daughter-in-law, Vaio
(Vi-o) and wife; but Mobi's anxiety and consideration reached not
only these, but all whose lives were now endangered.

The time for wise, quick, strenuous action had suddenly arrived
—a moment's delay would mean the loss of some or all of them. No
one realized this more than Mohi. He immediately called to each one,
name by name, and received an answer from all but the Spaniard.
When last seen he was sitting on the cabin; and, thinking that he might
have gone inside and was trapped there, Mohi dived under the ship and

entered the cabin, but it was so dark that he could see nothing, and was forced to return to the surface. Being an expert swimmer and diver, despite his sixty-odd years, he made several other attempts to find the lost man, by diving under and about the boat, but to no avail—the Spaniard was never seen again. He turned his attention to the remaining members of the party, still floundering among the raging billows and clinging to the edge of the ship or parts of the rigging, in darkness as that of the blind; and those who were unable to help themselves he assisted to a place of safety upon the side of the boat. He found the mother of the little boy struggling to save both herself and her child; the Chinaman was hanging to the main boom. But even when the probability of immediate death had been overcome, it was still a constant and strenuous task to hold on to the side of the overturned boat in so furious and wild a sea. Mohi's faith was not without works, however; he continued to use every means possible by which the safety of his friends might be secured. Diving into the sea again, he cut the jib sail loose, brought it to the top and tied it so as to break the force of the waves. He then made fast another rope over the side of the ship to which they all could cling and thus lessen the danger of being washed off into that surging, dashing, covetous monster of death. Now that everyone was secure and as comfortable as possible, Mohi took his stand on the keel at the stern of the ship, with a rope as support, and watched and swayed as the dark, dismal hours of night tolled off, until the break of day shed light upon the pathetic scene.

When day dawned the captain and Vaio suggested that the mast be removed, thinking the boat could then be righted. To such action, however, Mohi refused to accede, as he sensed the dangerous probability of losing mast, sails, ropes, anchors and all—and Mobi's judgment takes precedent over even a ship captain's in so grave a situation. But the captain and Vaio argued and insisted until, finally, Mohi consented. As the mast was loosened, a large wave struck the ship—the mast and all connected with it, together with part of the ship's flooring, were torn away. Mohi tried to tie them to the rear of the boat, but the rope was too short, and he was compelled to let them go—true to his premonition, all were lost. The ship was righted, but far more damage than good had been done. Their plight now was at the extreme— nothing left but a shell of a boat, and that filling with water.

They all sensed the apparent hopelessness of their predicament; but Mohi had reserved the greatest expression of his faith and hope till last. In that little company were Catholics, Protestants, Reorganites and Latter-day Saints. Mohi addressed them: "Of ourselves we can do no more; we are doomed; there is no way by which we may escape the grim spectre, Death, which is slowly but surely approaching, except through the help of God. This is no time for difference of opinion, or variety of religious thought. If you will unite your faith with mine, we will ask the Lord for help, and we shall be saved." They readily agreed. Mohi then asked his daughter-in-law, a member of the Reorganite church, to lead them in song, after which he prayed, with implicit faith and confidence, nothing wavering, to that God whom he had been taught to worship and to approach in time of need. Judging the time by the sun and the stars, they held such a prayer service at 6 a. m., 10 a. m., 3 p.m, and 9 p. m. of each day.

As each day came and went without sign of sail or help in any form, their plight increased—they were gradually sinking into oblivion. With no food, no water, no sustenance of any kind, they became weaker and weaker, but they still had faith and hope—at least Mohi did. On the fourth day, after the 8 o'clock prayer, the daughter-in-law said she had received a manifestation of some nature, in which she seemed to see two personages approaching the boat; the one dressed in black; the other, in white. As they reached the boat, the one in black went on; while the one in white stopped to view the situation, but disappeared as Mohi said, "Amen." The relating of this incident, whatever it was, gave new courage and life to the sufferers. It was a sign, they said, that they were to be saved.

The women now were physically unable to sing, but Mohi continued to pray at the appointed hours. The morning of the fifth day brought a calm sea, placid, unruffled; the Demon of the storm had spent his strength, and, thinking there was little more to do, had left the vanquished on the battlefield, apparently to die at leisure. The calm sea, however, permitted them to bail the water from their boat, thus raising it above the surface of the sea, and improving their condition somewhat. Great sharks swam leisurely about the boat, as if waiting for a tasty human morsel; but Mohi, unafraid, motivated by faith and the desire to appease their appetites and satisfy their curiosities, swam as leisurely among them, feeding them bits of copra from out his hands. Thus faith closed the mouths of sharks, as it had closed the mouths of lions.

In the afternoon of the fifth day, the Chinaman, whose faith apparently was no longer equal to the trial, became delirious and, in an attempt to jump overboard, fell into Mobi's arms and passed away. In the evening Mohi ordered them all to keep their places and to look straight ahead. He then took the Chinaman's body to the rear of the boat, prepared it as best he could for burial, dedicated the spot, and consigned the remains to an ocean grave. Having no weights to use, he feared the body would return to the surface; but as it was lowered into the sea, it took a downward course and disappeared. That night and the next day passed without much change, except that the increasing pangs of hunger and thirst added steadily to their emaciation.

As the seventh day of their plight dawned, a beautiful Sabbath morning, their cloud of despair showed a silver lining. When their boat was upset they were southwest from Makatea, but they had now drifted to the northeast, or leeward, side of that island. On the western horizon a dark speck took shape and as it increased in size, their hearts responded with a like increase in interest and anxiety. Was it but the sign of another impending storm? "A ship!" shouted Mohi; "'tis the smoke of a steamer." Those magic words caused a thrill and awakening of the little party, such as might be expected when Gabriel blows his trump on the morn of the resurrection. And such veritably it seemed to them. The exultation at the thought of possible rescue and prolonged life made them forget for the moment their misery and suffering. Mohi quickly took some boards from the boat, fastened them together, tied a cloth to the end, and frantically signalled—but to no avail. As the rays of the sun break through the density of a storm cloud for just a moment and then recede, so their little world was left again in gloom, darkness and despair.

*　*　*　*

The steamer was headed for Makatea. They had been at sea about twelve days, and all on board were now eagerly watching the island in the distance—the reason for their not seeing the drifing wreck on the port side of the ship.

*　*　*　*

They continued to place their trust in God; and Mohi prayed steadfastly for their relief and rescue, with faith that but few know. He also conducted religious service that Sunday morning, and encouraged his fellow-sufferers with quotations from the scriptures, wherein was shown the mercy and protection of God toward the prophets and saints of old in times of distress and danger. "By their faith were they saved," said Mohi, "and despite the apparent hopelessness of our situation, we must not give up; as long as there is life there is hope; only 'he that endureth to the end shall be saved.' "

The cries of the little boy for something to eat and drink, to which it was impossible for them to comply, were like knife-thrusts into the hearts of those loving, sympathetic people. His frail little tabernacle, being unequal to the ordeal of seven days without food or water, aggravated by wet and cold, began to crumble and break down. His little spirit, finding that tabernacle no longer a fit place in which to dwell, it appeared, was preparing to take its leave. Mohi dedicated him to the Lord, and with true mother-love the women huddled about him on the deck of the ship.

With the coming of night, there came a feeling of peace, calm, hope, joy. The tropic moon shone full and clear; with not a ripple on the ocean, nor the slightest breeze to break the stillness. As in the fields of Bethlehem, when the angels announced the birth of the Savior, so the very atmosphere surrounding them seemed filled with the announcement of something about to occur. Midnight approached. Most of the others were asleep; but Mohi sat by himself and—waited. For some time he had been watching a dark object in the distant west. He said nothing of it to the others; he wondered if it were just his imagination; an illusion, perhaps. It appeared to be approaching, nearer and nearer. Still he said nothing; the men of the party had made the threat that they would swim for the first thing that looked like land or ship, and a danger lay in their emaciated condition; then, too, he knew that to arouse them with a false hope would tend to destroy rather than to buoy up their faith. Another half hour of almost breathless suspense passed; he was hoping to see a light, but only the stars and moon gave semblance of what he sought.

But there! there! He rubbed his eyes. Was he dreaming? No, there it was—a red light! Out of the abundance of his heart his mouth spoke—he thanked the Lord! He then broke the news. The sleepers awoke with a start; excitement reigned supreme. They wanted to jump into the ocean and swim to the oncoming vessel; but Mohi restrained them. He knew that seven days of constant peril, without either food or drink, had robbed them of the necessary endurance for such a feat. "Save your energy," he counseled, "and when the time is right we will all join in a call of distress."

On came the ship—a steamer. But, see! It was heading straight for the little craft! What did it mean? Were they to be destroyed after all? There seemed almost a cessation of heartbeats for the second. Ah! It veered to the left and continued ahead. Now, together. "Ship ahoy!" rang out as one voice, clear and resonant, over the shimmering, placid sea. Could it be that they had not heard? They would likely all be asleep, except the watch, at this time of night. There was no sign of response—the ship sped past and on. Hope began to die. But why was it making that turn to the right? Ah, could it be? They waited breathlessly. The vessel was returning. Mohi urged them to call again. As their anxious cry again broke the stillness of the night, the searchlights of the steamer began to play upon the surface of the sea. They had heard. The source of the weird night-call was soon located, the life boat quickly lowered, and the little party of distressed souls taken aboard. The remains of the craft on which they had weathered the worst was left behind.

*   *   *   *

Upon the arrival of the steamer at Makatea that Sunday morning, the captain explained later, they found several ships ahead of them. This meant a delay of a few days before they could get their load of phosphate. There being no suitable place at which to drop anchor, the captain decided to cruise around in the open sea at the leeward side of the island. He set the compass, left an officer in charge of the wheel and retired to his room. Without any apparent reason, however, he returned to the wheel and ordered the course changed more to the left, and retired again. But he felt queer, nervous, restless—he was unable to sleep. He returned to the deck again and sat down beside the wheel. Suddenly and impulsively he grasped the wheel and gave it a mighty spin, which caused the ship to swerve quickly to the left; then held it again to a straight course. He started again for his room; but stopped—and listened. What was that, a cry of distress? He asked the man at the wheel if he heard anything. The officer answered that it sounded like someone calling. "Turn the ship around," was the command; and the big vessel was soon heading in the opposite direction. The call sounded again from the surface of the deep—there was no mistake this time—and the searchlights were soon able to say, "There they are."

The people of the steamer were English, and the natives told their story by means of signs and a few words of French, which Vaio and one of the ship's men could speak and understand. Many kinds of tempting food were placed before them; but the ship's doctor ordered it taken away, and regulated their diet to suit their condition. The

ON CAME THE SHIP—A STEAMER. MOHI THANKED THE LORD

doctor also took charge of the little boy, in whom the flame of life still flickered, but it shortly afterwards died out.

The rescued party were taken to the island of Makatea, where friends ministered to their needs. Thus had their faith been tested, and, being of the quality "that endureth to the end," had brought them deliverance and prolonged life.

Do Spare This Tree

Oh, Forestry, do spare this tree!
An emblem of eternity,
That bathes in light with one applause
To all of God's eternal laws,
And sighs to all who call, "Be free."

Oh, faithful wonder, ancient tree,
Partaker of all purity!
If we could live to your great age
And still retain a cleanly page,
How great our glory then would be.

Mink, Creek, Idaho.

Oh, famous, patient, ancient tree,
Master of humility!
The frosty years throughout your days
Were also met with Summer's blaze;
But living law has held you free.

Oh, Forestry, do spare this tree,
An emblem of eternity.
Perhaps, if left here all unmarred,
May live to see our coming Lord.
Oh, Forestry, do spare this tree.

CHRISTEN HANSEN.

Explaining the likeness to a companion—the resemblance to the *Sacred Ankh,* * of Egypt. Carved on the rocks near Deseret.

TO THE ANCIENT INDIAN HIEROGLYPHICS
A Community Holiday Outing

BY FRANK BECKWITH

"See, my dear," the young lady to the left is saying, "here is the carving the lecturer spoke of; here is the object near the hand, just as he said. To denote it as belonging near or in the hand, the man who carved it in the long ago drew the bar of the design crossing the man's wrist. And compared with the text book illustration, there is certainly a resemblance, when one's attention is called to it. What did he say it was?"

"He said it was a very curious likeness to the ankh, which is the combined circle and cross so frequently pictured in the hands of figures carved on the obelisks of ancient Egypt," said the one who was questioned.*

The young lady to the left was a visitor from Salt Lake City, spending a week with her hostess, who is sitting on the right. The occasion was a holiday outing held one day last fall when a throng of about three hundred persons gathered among the lava boulders southwest of Deseret, in Millard county, to study the ancient Indian hieroglyphics found there. A lecturer took each of the carved rocks, and drew out to the fullest extent the interest in each; some he found to contain figures and designs resembling Old World usage. This rock, and one other, so strikingly illustrated the similarity as to carry conviction that the intent of the person who carved it in the long ago was to use a likeness of a known historical symbol.

"It is well known,' said the lecturer, "that scholars boldly assert that not only one, but several waves or groups of immigrants may have

*The Egyptian cross with a handle (*Ankh Ansata*) is the *sign of life*. Its presence in Central and North American lore and monuments is said to be proof of connection with the Old World.—Ed.

come to North America from the Old World.   The most common course for that journey is usually thought of as being via Behring Strait, by boat or upon the ice floes—or by way of the chain of the Aleutian Islands.   Some scholars find in the South American natives so strong a similarity to Malayan features as to lead them to say that Polynesian seamen may have come from those islands to the coast of South America.

"History does not record any proved or accepted visitation anciently of any people to the shores of either American continent who came directly across the Pacific,—that is, accepted in the sense of secular history, not religious record.

"But such a passage is not difficult of belief; especially when one bears in mind that the direct passage has been made across, in a manner most noteworthy.   Harry Pigeon circumnavigated the world in a thirty-four foot boat, sailing alone.   And again the similar feat was done when Captain Slocum made the passage of the Pacific in the small boat called *The Spray*.

"From the weight of indisputable evidences," continued the speaker of the occasion, "scholars do accept that a wave or waves, a group or groups, may have come to these shores.   And you," he said, addressing his audience, "accept the passage of Lehi."

Continuing his remarks, the speaker said:

"The very oldest, the primal, urge of man is self-expression.   People of all nations have sought to say something, and to put that expression into permanent form.   In Persia, Assyria, Chaldea, Greece, Rome, Egypt—human nature was the same.   Convenient rocks were carved with a message; that message may have been a narrative of deeds of glory, a recital of events in a great monarch's reign, or the vainglory of an ambitious ruler;—but whatever the content, the act was the expression of human nature the world over.   The motivation was ever the same.

"The red man obeyed the same urge.

"Indian hieroglyphics were cut for a similar reason.   Though our efforts are baffled for an interpretation (though no Rosetta Stone or other paralleled passages gives us a clue), the basic intent, be it monumental inscription in Eurasia, or an Indian petroglyph in Utah, was and is always the same,—a message—a message of some kind with intent to express to another a thought represented by the marks."

Establishing a foundation by the preceding remarks, the speaker continued:

"We have now come to the pith of the matter.   Establishing that persons arrived here, be the manner of their coming what it may, be their passage by the north or south or straight across, the purpose of our meeting here today is to bring out, by studious scrutiny, any plausible or acceptable likeness of a usage here with a known historical usage in the Old World.

"Two such instances of similarity are found in these ancient carvings.

"On a rock cut with several figures in ideagraphic expression appears an object held in the left hand, which is strikingly similar to the *crux ansata* or *'sacred ankh'* of the Egyptians."

(That figure may be identified in the photo as the ideagraph with the large circle for head, straight stem for body, with legs drawn from it and arms on each side; the left arm is seen to end with a circle surmounting a cross.)

"In the old Egyptian usage this emblem is always held in the hand of the god, by the fingers passing into the loop of the circle.

"Were this the only instance of this similarity to be found here at Deseret, it might very properly be classed as merely a rare coin-

Top: Ideagraph combined with picturegraphic methods of thought presentation. Placed almost in the hand of the man to the left is a wondrous likeness to the *Ankh* or *crux ansata* of the Egyptians.
Bottom: A close-up, and a hand drawing taken from a text-book on Egyptology. Compare the two.

cidence, a chance happening, to which no value should be given. But on the contrary, the similarity is found twice.

"The second occurrence is on the left of a group of rather varied extent. Because of the number of the figures, this entire group was probably written with a narrative intent.

"The crude artisan, doing the best he could (and that best was woefully deficient), drew a figure of a man out of proportion to the rest of the group. It is much larger than any of the other figures. He failed to attain due proportion; nor did he have the skill to draw, as being held in the hand, the object which his tradition or his slight remembrance told him should be held in the hand. But, doing the best he could, he drew the object just as near the required position as he could; he further indicated his intent by extending the bar of his design across the wrist of the figure of the man, denoting by that means that it belonged to and had to do with the hand of the figure. Had he the ability to have drawn in better proportion, had he adhered to proper comparative size, the circle would have been held in the hand; but if, in his error of proportion, he had done so, there would not have been room—the legs would have been in the way for a design of even one-third the size he used."

* * * *

This was the figure the girls were studying. The camera caught them going over the details of the lecture, discussing it point by point. The visiting lady was Miss Esther Nokelby; her hostess on that day was Miss Elva Mace, whose father is a veritable mine of information about things Indian, and of the wonders to be found in that vicinity. He acts as guide for many parties who seek first-hand information from the objects of interest themselves.

One large visiting group placed itself before the big carved stone, which has been named "The First Issue of the Deseret News," and were photographed with that in the background. In the group were Bishop and Mrs. E. L. Lyman, of Delta; Samuel Western, age eighty-two; Lee R. Cropper, also age eighty-two, both from Deseret. That day Mr. Cropper said, "I have seen these rock carvings as far back as fifty-two years ago, and never have they lost their interest to me.'

John Bennett of Deseret acted as chairman, and was one of the speakers. He took as his subject the great natural phenomenon of the stone face, which by his oratory was christened "The Guardian of Deseret." He stood before the throng, head bared, and rose to rhetorical flights as he brought out how that wonderful stone face must have seen civilizations come to this land; had seen their rise and fall; had witnessed the massacre of the "Little People of the Cliffs;" had looked upon the vicissitudes of Aztec and Inca; and joyed in the joys of Lehi's descendants and sorrowed in their sorrows.

Many of his hearers stood rapt in attention, with faces turned toward the great stone face, as he drew his simile. Others of his listeners bowed their heads in reveries of deepest thought, pondering over a subject which is fraught with so much interest.

Delta, Utah.

READING THE BOOK OF MORMON

[To encourage the reading of the Book of Mormon, the *Improvement Era* in November offered to the winning M Man a two-years' subscription to the *Era* for the best five-hundred-word statement and application on the "Waters of Sebus;" and for the second and third-best stories, each a one-year's subscription.

LaVern Wilkinson, Third ward M Men class, North Weber stake, won first place; Perry D. Whittle, Fairview, Franklin stake, Idaho, won second place; and Hans Schotel, Rotterdam, Netherlands conference, third place. The writers will please let the editor know to what address to send the *Era*, and the magazine will be forwarded promptly.

The response was not as general as we a•ticipated; therefore, we make another offer to the M Men throughout the Church, with a further view to encourage the reading of the Book of Mormon:

For the best five-hundred-word story and application, connected with the "Waters of Mormon," (p. 168-8, 183-18, 205-3) written by an M Man, a two-years' subscription to the *Era* will be given; and for the second and third-best stories, a one-year's subscription, each. The writings must be sent to the editors by the first day of March, 1927. Each paper must give the name and address of the writer, and the ward M Man class of which he is a member. You are invited to write, and we should have a thousand papers by March 1, 1927.—*Editors.*]

WATERS OF SEBUS

BY LaVERN WILKINSON, THIRD WARD M MEN CLASS,
NORTH WEBER

Ammon, one of the sons of Mosiah who rejected the right to the kingly office to become preachers of righteousness, was journeying at one time as a missionary among his brethren, the Lamanites, in the land of Nephi. The Lamanites were "wild and a hardened and a ferocious people." They murdered the Nephites to rob and plunder, deeming it right to gain riches in this way rather than by righteous labor.

Soon after entering the land of Ishmael, Ammon was taken bound before Lamoni, king of the Lamanites. The king was to decide whether Ammon should live or die. Ammon gained favor with the king and was allowed to live and become his servant. He was sent to guard the flocks of the king, as they grazed near, and were watered at, the "Waters of Sebus."

On the third day of his service, certain of the Lamanites scattered his flocks, insomuch that the shepherds were hard pressed to gather them. The gathering was accomplished under the leadership of Ammon, and they returned again to Sebus. As they approached, Ammon went forth to meet the enemy. With God-given power, singlehanded, he defeated them. Having smitten off the arms of many and slain a few with his slingshot, he caused the remainder to flee. A report was carried to the king, who was pleased with the great service Ammon had rendered in the protection of his flocks. He recognized the power of Ammon and gave him permission to preach throughout the land.

This instance of God blessing man with miraculous power is the result of man's obedience to God. In this chapter we are told of three laws that Ammon obeyed to gain such great favor with God:

First: In the second verse of the seventeenth chapter of Alma we read of Mosiah's sons: "For they were men of sound understanding, and they had searched the scriptures diligently, that they might know the word of God." Thus we see that man must first prepare by diligent study for the work of the Lord.

Second: We are told in the third verse, "They had given themselves to much prayer, and fasting; therefore, they had the spirit of prophecy, and the spirit of revelation, and when they taught, they taught with the power and authority of God." Also, because of prayer, Ammon was given power to overthrow his enemies. Thus to knowledge gained, we add the power of God, by prayer and fasting.

Third: We find Ammon and his brethren had the desire of service. This is shown in the fourth verse, which relates that they had been teaching the word of God to the Lamanites for the space of fourteen years, causing many to turn from their sins, and come to a knowledge of the truth.

Ammon possessed the knowledge of God, gained by preparation; the Spirit and power of God, through prayer and fasting; and the desire to use these in the service of God and his fellowmen. He was thus enabled to gain favor with the king and to open his entire domain to the teaching of the word of God for the salvation of souls.

By preparation, by prayer, by fasting, and through a desire to serve, we may, like Ammon and his brothers, be a power for good among our fellowmen.

Ogden, Utah

That Boy of Ours

If we could have our wish, could know, and feel,
That boy of ours is clean, and pure, and strong;
If we could be assured that he is safe,
Then in our hearts there'd always be a song.

If we could know that he is brave, and true,
Fighting with the side of truth and right,
If we could feel that he is JUST A MAN,
Then would our hearts be thrilled, with true delight,

If we could know that he is going straight,
That as a boy, and man, he'll win the game
Of life, that each of us must play,
Our hearts would then rejoice to hear his name.

Moab, Utah   F. M. SHAFER

AN INTERNATIONAL: SCIENCE CONGRESS

How the World can be made a Paradise for its Inhabitants

BY DR. FRANKLIN S. HARRIS, PRESIDENT OF BRIGHAM YOUNG
UNIVERSITY

Time was when it was thought that the only way a person or
nation could rise was by the fall of some other individual or group——
a sort of "one-man's-pleasure- is-another-man's-pain" idea.

This idea is rapidly being cast into the waste heap. We are
coming to realize that two men may make a trade without one of
them being cheated; they may both be benefited by the exchange.
Likewise the fall of one nation may not benefit others; in fact, bad
conditions in one country are sure to cause adverse situations in other
countries as well. For example, an outbreak of a serious contagious
disease in Canada or Mexico cannot but be a menace to the people
of the United States.

With the development of modern science, it is becoming clear
that the truth should be the sole possession of no individual or group;
it should be available to all men as soon as it is discovered. In
line with this idea we have many international organizations whose
purpose is to foster the interchange of knowledge so that the discoveries of any scientist living in any country may be available to all
of the people of the entire world.

If a Japanese scientist should discover the methods of treating
some disease, such as leprosy, he would not be doing his duty as a
scientist if he kept his knowledge to himself and treated only the few
lepers in his vicinity. The modern point of view calls on him to
make known to all men his findings so that all lepers everywhere may
be helped by his treatment.

I have just attended one of these international gatherings which
was held in Japan. It was the third Pan-Pacific Science Congress.
Its purpose was to consider particularly the problems of countries bor-
dering the Pacific ocean. It is a well known fact that most of the
more advanced countries, scientifically, are situated around the north
Atlantic ocean, and as a result most attention is given to the scientific
problems of this area. This means that some of the problems of other
sections are likely to be neglected. For example, this Atlantic area is
all in the humid part of the world; whereas, more than half of the
total land area of the world comes in zones of low rainfall.

These Pacific Science Congresses are held every three years. The
first session met in Hawaii, the second in Australia, and this last
one in Japan. In each case the country in which the congress is
held acts as host and pays the expenses.

A limited number of scientists are invited from each participating
country, through its National Research Council. These are selected

Photo by F. S. Harris

ONE OF JAPAN'S BEAUTY SPOTS, MIYAJIMA

with a view of having authorities covering the major scientific problems of the Pacific area. My own invitation came because of my knowledge of the agriculture of arid sections.

The United States led in number of over-seas delegates, with thirty-five members; next came Australia with twenty-two, the Netherlands, East Indies, New Zealand, Hawaii, Philippines, China, Russia, Malay States, Great Britain, France, Canada, and a few other countries. Japan had practically all of her scientific workers on hand to receive the benefits of the discussions.

The more formal part of the congress covered two weeks, but there were many excursions both before and after the meetings to points of scientific interest, so that more than a month was covered altogether.

The congress was divided into many sections according to subject matter and papers on similar subjects were grouped together. From the program I take the following sections: Biological Sciences, (General), Physical Sciences, (General), Agriculture, Geography, Architecture (for earth-quake proof construction), Astronomy, Botany, Hygiene and Medicine, Seismology, Geology, Zoology and Fishery, Anthropology and Ethnology, and Radio Waves.

The Pacific ocean—its currents and life—earthquakes, and volcanoes, came in for much discussion since these are very live questions in Japan.

Chairmen were elected for the various sections. I had the honor of being elected chairman of the section of Agriculture. All the proceedings were carried on in English. The only variation from this was when the Japanese princes spoke in Japanese and some of the French delegates spoke part of the time in French. They are not entirely willing to have English take the place of the international language which was held so long by the French.

One could not go through this congress without being impressed by the oneness of mankind and by the similarity of the problems of all lands.   One is overwhelmed at the perfectly marvelous advances which are being made in the various branches of science.   Conditions which formerly held down mankind are now being eliminated and the world is become a much more desirable place in which to live than it has ever been during the history of man.

I was surprised to see how thoroughly united are the scientists of all countries.   Truly science knows no bounds, such as color of

Photo by F. S. Harris
SCIENTISTS IN BOTANICAL GARDENS, SAPPORO, JAPAN

skin, or geographical boundary.   It is for all men, regardless of race, religion, political affiliation, wealth, or previous condition of servitude; its benefits are world-wide and it will gradually help to melt away national hatreds and contention arising from differences of religious and political beliefs.

• Science aims at the discovery of the truth, and its methods are the best way that man has devised to separate truth from error.   Of course, many mistakes are made by workers in science, but by the use of rigorous scientific methods these will gradually be discovered and corrected.

Japan demonstrated herself to be the best of hosts.   She is a little more ceremonious than we Americans are used to, but if this goes with real politeness it is doubtless a good thing.   The country was at its best, and that is saying a good deal.   I had an opportunity to see nearly all parts of it and I was charmed by its beauty and impressed by the order which I found everywhere.

I came from this congress more strongly convinced than ever that when nations cease their useless contentions, when individuals are willing to put in the background a part of. their selfishness, when all will work together for the good of all, and when that part of the energy of people which is now spent in contention is diverted to the discovery of truth in a scientific manner, the world can be made a veritable paradise for its inhabitants.

On U. S. S. *President Van Buren*, between Manila and Singapore, November 27, 1926

Throughout All Eternity

(Dedicated to my Sons and Daughters)

I stood at the marriage altar,
   Two heads were in silence bowed—
With terror my heart-beats falter
   In dread of the priest's black shroud.
His ritual, so-deep and smothered,
   Struck me like an arrow's dart;—
"Do you two now take each other
   E'en until death shall you part?"

"And do you now take this woman?"
   Came accents so cold and terse,
"And you, too, this man, in common,
   For better or for worse?
To honor, to love, and cherish,
   Through all of life's joys and pains?
The tie that binds you to perish
   When your life no more remains?"

"I do," thus replied the woman.
   "I do," so replied the man.
"Then take thou this ring as omen
   Of faith throughout life's short span—
A band just to bind each other.
   Though only for this short life—"
And now, as a Priest and Brother,
   I pronounce you man and wife."

The spirit within me trembles,
   I lift up mine eyes above,
How can these earthly made symbols
   Curtail thus a heaven-made love?
And why in the Realms Supernal
   Cannot these two souls still live,
United for aye, eternal,
   Through Him who has power to give?

The veil of deep darkness opens,
   The mists now fall from mine eyes,
A voice from the heavens hath spoken
   And edict from out the skies;
The clouds up above me sever;
   In Realms far beyond I see:—
"I NOW SEAL YOU TWO FOREVER,
THROUGHOUT ALL ETERNITY."

C. C. BUSH

WESTERNERS IN ACTION

By Harrison R. Merrill

One would naturally suppose that snowballs and peaches would not grow well in the same orchard; that flower contests and dog races could not be held in the same town, but one would be mistaken. In Provo the winter fruitage and the winter sports are as interesting and as hotly contested as those of the summer.

"The call of the wild" was heard by nearly forty boys this winter when Dell Webb, city recreational director, issued a notice that the annual dog races would be held during the last week of December. For months silent lads had been running behind their sleds and wagons training for just such an occasion, but they were as close-mouthed about it as Esquimaux or—Tud Kent.

Twenty-two boys entered dogs in the dog derby, and ten others were on hand ready for the races when the old town clock indicated the time for the starting of the first race. The recreational director was prepared for a last-minute jam and, therefore, allowed all who had a dog and a sled to enter.

The judges measured off the distance and the races began. Although a few dog fights ensued when the thirty-two dogs began to scrap acquaintance with one another, the order was much better than it was a few years ago when Mr. Webb introduced the races. At that time an onlooker couldn't be sure whether the occasion was a dog race, a dog fight, or merely dog meat.

I have seen dogs run with sleighs who seemed to think it a terrible bore, to say the least, if not a great imposition. I was greatly surprised and pleased this year, therefore, when the dogs took to the races with as much gusto as the drivers themselves—in most cases. There were a few canines, of course, who revealed their dog natures at every angle. I met one lad with a fine-looking, up-standing dog.

"Why isn't he in the race?" I asked.

"He won't pull," the boy replied, disgustedly. "He's big enough and fast enough to win, but he just won't go."

I felt sorry for the kiddie as well as for the dog. Somehow I felt that the team hadn't got together.

The Grand Slam, an original name given to an original race by the Recreational Director, was the biggest of the events. Practically every boy entered this race. It was to be the longest of the day, and was to be wide open. There were no rules except that the boy and the sled and the dog had to cover the distance. It didn't matter whether the dog pulled the boy or whether the boy pulled the dog. Before seeing the race, I thought that perhaps the winner would actually pull his dog, but when I saw those canines get out and "dust," I discovered that no fellow could win that way.

One boy had that race practically won, but seemed to be unaware that he could help his steed over the line. His dog made a beautiful run up and back, but just before he crossed the tape, which was in the center of a crowd which lined both sides of the race track, Mr. Dog sat down on his haunches and refused to budge, until after Blaine Farley and his white dog shot by and over the line in time to win the race.

It was a great day for the boys, a great day for the dogs, and a

Top: Some of the entrants. Blaine and his dog are fourth from the left.
Bottom: Winners receiving prizes.

great day for Provo city. As I saw the youths surrounding the Director, eager to secure their prizes, I thought what a capital idea the Snowball Derby really is. Due to the liberality of Provo merchants and to the industry of Mr. Webb, they all got prizes. I think I could recommend it as an opportunity for any community that has more than one boy and one dog.

Provo, Utah

BY WAY OF COMPENSATION

By John Q. Adams

The irregular tread of a thousand feet brought consternation to the denizens of the desert, as the cavalcade crept wearily along. Five hundred stern-visaged, silent marchers had set their pace, and the children of Nature stepped quickly aside to let them pass. Countless lizards stampeded this way and that; while a gaunt coyote, poised in surveillance, betimes shrilled out a nerve-racking monologue.

It was late afternoon, the hour of dead calm. The contact of foot, hoof and wheel with the sand and alkali made a cloud of vapory, choking dust. At intervals, patches of dwarf cactus or challenging sentries of the gigantic species succeeded easily in deflecting the line of march, for bare, bleeding flesh is no match for the merciless spine of the prickly pear. The coaxing "git up" of the teamsters at the rear gave way eventually to the more effective whang of the four-lash rawhide.

As the sun came in contact with the horizon, the blast of a bugle, clear, sudden, resonant, shattered the dread silence into quavering vibrations, and instantly each animate unit of the company came to a standstill. The spot was selected simply because of the fact that the approaching twilight rendered a halt imperative, not that it had any special features distinguishing it as a good camping place.

Instead of the naturally expected move for immediate rest, numbers of these weather-beaten soldiers set busily to excavating in several places with pick and shovel, as if their very lives depended upon the rapidity with which the holes were made. And such, indeed, was the case. They had gone for days without trace of water on the surface; and, as each evening came, it was either dig or remain thirsty.

Night soon reigned supreme; stars of varying brilliancy danced and quivered; while the moon, mounting higher and higher toward the zenith of her throne, piloted her way among her stellar offspring. On all sides the peculiar night noises of the desert, subdued yet impressive, mingled low and indistinct in a soothing medley.

Through it all Jethro Williams lay, his quiet, deep musing in strict accord with the surrounding restfulness of nature; and yet, as if for the purpose of mere emphasis or contrast, his thought grew exceedingly tumultuous at times, as the gnawing pangs of an unappeased hunger prodded him to wakefulness. The usual, simple expedient of a belt taken up, hole by hole, as hunger made its inroad, failed utterly now to replace something substantial.

With the approach of midnight, unable longer to endure it in silence, he quietly left his blankets, stepped over and between forms more restful than himself, and soon reached the solitary sentry, who stood leaning upon his musket for friendly support. Making his identity known by the necessary pass-word, he left the confines of the

camp and soon found himself far beyond the last wagon. His somewhat aimless strides reminded him harshly of the fact that his bare
feet, coming in contact with unnoticed cactus, were lacerated and
swollen, and to proceed farther was an impossibility. He sank to the
ground with added pain, his mind a whirl of conflicting emotions; and
then— a new thought—by some sudden transformation, things became
different.

The light had broken through his mental lethargy and miscon-
ception, as the sun's unconquered rays break suddenly through the
sullen cloud-banks; and Jethro was soon engaged in fervent, simple
prayer. The Infinite always responds to man's earnest appeal; and,
just as manna and quail and buffalo had often appeared before the
eyes of Faith, so this man gazed with surprised delight upon a large
hare not ten paces away. A quickly sent pistol ball found its mark in
the equally surprised, long-eared visitor, and hope passed from a dying
ember to the glow of reality—Jethro's entire field of endeavor was
lighted up.

His first impulse was to appease his hunger then and there, but,
restraining himself, he returned to camp. As he brushed past a covered wagon dignified by the word "Hospital," a harrowing groan of
agony, mingled with execrations, informed him of the condition of the
sole patient. Another half dozen steps would have taken him beyond
the sound of the occupant's wail, but a piercing cry rang in his ears,
"Food, food, only a bite!"

Now was fought the battle in which hosts of mortals are vanquished each hour of every passing day—the fight of self. To lay
down one's life willingly amid the glamour and stress of battle is not
unusual; but in the isolation and secrecy of the heart—to quell the
rebellion of every force within, and repel invasion from every quarter
without, and all in calm, cold premeditation, devoid of the stimulus
of attack, wherein men lose their identity in the frenzied heat of
charges and counter-charges—there is the real battleground of life!

Jethro Williams was now in the thick of that fight. Was he not
on the verge of collapse himself, through scanty fare and almost super-
human exertion? Had he not endeavored with his whole mental power,
the last few days, to inveigle his unwary sense into the forlorn belief
that the strips of rawhide which had formed the entire basis of the
thin, tasteless fluid called "soup" were really strips of juicy, palatable
beef or mutton? And now that he had been fortunate above his
companions in securing so invaluable a trophy as that dangling from his
hand, why should he deny himself this sustenance that seemed so necessary in preventing the grim specter, Death, from knocking at his own
door? And he recalled also that this particular man, more than all
others in the company, for some mysterious, indefinable reason, had
appeared to him the very antithesis of all that goes to make men in any
way companionable. Never a word had passed between them; never
had either acted hostile or otherwise toward the other; and yet Jethro,
from the moment they left the banks of the Missouri, had entertained

a growing feeling that somehow, somewhere, they two would find themselves in an unusual relationship—and not a congenial one either.

He stood in the dark, hesitating; and then, with a determination born of the faith by which he had become possessed of the priceless treasure, and as one in a dream, he raised the canvas on the darker side of the wagon, and deftly swung the limp bundle of fur and flesh into the bunk of the delirious occupant; and silently stole to his own tattered blankets.

* * *

California in '49! What romance, adventure, accomplishments and varied experiences weave themselves with fascination around this simple phrase. On a rough bunk of slabs covered with dried grass, in one of the dirt-roofed cabins that made up San Francisco in that magic year, lay Jethro Williams, weak and emaciated, his haggard features hid behind a shaggy beard. He had come to San Francisco from Southern California after his discharge from the army, and had joined in the activities of the day—the great game of chance—and, apparently, had lost.

A gaunt, raw-boned, bewhiskered individual sat on a small stool beside the bunk, his legs crossed, in deep, silent meditation. Quietness reigned, not even the ticking of a clock obtruding itself. With an introductory cough, the man shifted his position to a more comfortable attitude, and began speaking in deep, measured tones.

"Well, pal, I reckon you are wondering what is coming next. I came in with the doctor for a purpose—it was easier that way; and now that he's gone I must give a reason for coming; and for staying, too, I suppose. I'm somewhat mixed in my thoughts and don't know just where to begin, but I have a score to settle with you, and you are expected to lie still, too, without a word."

The younger man turned a wondering gaze towards the speaker, but with no opportunity of reading there the thoughts of his unexpected visitor. Behind so grim and invulnerable a breastwork might be safely intrenched, without detection, either danger or favor. So he interposed no word, as the speaker continued with the object of his visit.

"Just fifteen years ago I moved into old Missouri with my wife and baby—a happy man. The year we arrived there fever took the mother, and I was left with little, two-year-old Lexie, the only thing in the whole world for which to live. The child and I made a pretty fair trial at enjoying life until she entered her 'teens; and I began to fear the day that someone might take her from me. Of course, such a thought had never occurred to her. We had a large clearing there in the wilderness, and at harvest time several men were needed to help us.

"One day two preachers came to our cabin and asked for a meal. I told them to line up with the crew, provided they tell what their business was in that neck o' the woods. They said their business there was to tell us something of vital importance, and that our asking them about it made their duty easier; but said they would rather wait until after we had eaten, and then explain it while we were resting in the shade; and they said that for the bread I gave them they would give us the 'bread of life.' 'Certainly, sir,' I replied, 'every person to his likin', but I can't get the meanin' of the bread o' life from you two.'

"My little girl had prepared the dinner, and had gone to lie down in the room we had arranged in the attic, as she was suffering with a headache. The passing of victuals had only commenced when a quarrel arose between two of the hands sitting at opposite sides of the table. This was not their first altercation, as a smothered animosity had rankled in their bosoms for a long time, but now all reserve was cast aside; and before we realized what was happening, a puff of smoke filled the room, and one of the men lay dead. The men grabbed the other fellow, to prevent him from shooting anybody else. 'Hold on there, fellows;' he yelled, 'before God, I swear I didn't pull a trigger. The preacher there was the man with the shootin' irons. Didn't you see the gun in his hands?' All eyes were turned toward the accused, as he replied, 'Yes, I did have a gun in my hand, but it was while struggling to wrest it from your murderous grasp! Search me, if you desire; you'll find that my only weapon is my Bible.' One of the men put his hand into the preacher's pocket, and instead of a Bible he pulled out a smoking pistol. 'A pretty looking Bible;' I exclaimed, 'one that will either convert or kill, I reckon.'

"Well, I suppose old Jake got what he deserved all right, but it was murder just the same, and it looked like the preacher had done the shooting. There was nothing else to do but turn him over to the sheriff; so we left one of the men to guard the preachers, while the remainder of us scattered to get the sheriff, the coroner and others. I was the first one back, and I found the guard bound and the prisoners gone.

"That wouldn't have been so bad if things had gone only that far, but—oh! I can't stand it; I can't stand to see that sight again!"

The narrator paused, turned in his seat and drew a sleeve across his shaggy brow. For some moments he gazed into space, entirely oblivious, apparently, to his surroundings. Making a mighty effort to control himself, he proceeded in a husky, broken voice.

"I called Lexie, but no answer came, and jumping up the ladder into the attic I saw a sight that, night or day, has never been erased from my mind. Lexie lay dead, shot by the second bullet that ranged up while the tussle for the gun was going on.

"I swore vengeance on the preacher, for I felt sure that the vermin with the gun in his pocket had done the deed; of course, perhaps without meaning to, but what's the difference when the end is the same? Without waiting a day after the girl was buried, I followed the preacher, and in the course of time learned that he was a 'Mormon' from over the country; so I made my way to the place on the Missouri where his people were bunched like sheep. After a time, by keeping somewhat under cover, I learned that the man I was after had just died, leaving a widow and an only son. The government at that time.

only three years ago, though it seems a lifetime to me, was fighting
Mexico, and called on the 'Mormons' for five hundred young men to go
to the front. , The boy had joined the company, and, though I felt
in every part of my body that I must kill the son of my girl's murderer,
I planned to do it some other day—always on some future day—for the
proper time, when I could torture him with the story of his father's
deed and then wipe out the account, had not presented itself when the
company of five hundred was ready to leave. So I also joined, as a
teamster in the supply train, and we started west. My, how I gloated
over my revenge, and how hellish were my plans!

"Well, we marched and marched for months, and my one big
chance hadn't come when we struck starvation and the like, half way
or more on the desert, and then I became terribly sick.

"One night, my doctor said, when I lay cussing and raving,
having had nothing to eat but leather soup for days, the wagon cover
was lifted, and—"

A sharp, piercing cry came from the sick man, as he bolted upright in his bunk, with hands pressed to his head, and staring at the
narrator with eyes fixed in horror and fright.

"And that was you?" cried Jethro, all his premonitions of evil
concerning this man coming back like a flash. "It's all a lie!" he
shouted. "Have you been driving your horrible story into my heart,
knowing you had me at bay, intending that I should be the means of
settling the account you claim? It isn't true, I, I—." He sank back
exhausted.

"Well, as I was going to say," continued the narrator, now by
far the calmer of the two, "a big, fine rabbit came sailing into the
wagon. The fellow who did it thought he was mighty cunning, but
enough of the candle light fell upon his face to let the doctor see who he
was; and, of course, you know the rest.

"Now, pal, you and I traveled from the Missouri in that company, and more than once I could see that you looked on me as a
peculiar fellow; and why shouldn't you, for you were sure enough
marked for the sacrifice. If ever a thunder clap came from a clear sky,
it was that act of yours· that night; and I could never again bring
myself to think along the line that had so constantly occupied my
mind and heart.

"So we brought up, or part of us did, at San Diego, and I met a
man there, on his dying bed, who told me something of great importance both to you and to me.. ˙He was the man left to guard the
preachers the day of the shooting, and he surely cleared the accused
preacher with his story of coaxing them to escape, because he knew they
were innocent. 'You know, I felt sorry for those preachers,' he said,
'because I saw the whole fracas, and they were no more guilty than I
was. That fellow slipped the gun into the preacher's pocket as soon
as he fired, and I was the only one, apparently, who saw the trick. I
didn't dare to say anything, because I might have been corpse number
two, with no gun to back up my words. So when we were alone I

told them they'd be doing the square thing to get out of there before the others returned, because it didn't make any difference if they were innocent, old Bill and his bunch would fix them just the same, as that was exactly the kind of law under which they were living there at that time, I told them that I would be able sometime to clear them, but not under the circumstances then existing. I finally persuaded them to tie me up and go. They got into the canoe at the edge of the river and dropped down stream, and I have never seen them since.' "

Rising to his feet, the relentless pursuer drew a small sack from his pocket.

"Only a few words more, pal," he said. "You see, I've been chasing you for nothing. You're on your back now and have had bad luck since coming here. I've done better. Back in the mountains where your people were headed three years ago, you have a mother. I know from reports that your people have arrived and settled there. As a small offering to balance our account, here is a little yellow dust to help you on your trip back there."

Ignoring the attempted apologies and profuse thanks of the sick man, the grim-visaged westerner dropped the small wallet on the bunk, took Jethro's hand, gazed for a moment into his face, and in silent emotion strode from the room.

Centerville, Utah.

My Span of Years

God gave to me my span of years,
A journey fraught with smiles and tears,
That I might learn to take his hand
And reach, by faith, a fairer land,
That I might strive to do his will,
A worthy mission to fulfil.

God gave to me my little span
That I might do the good I can,
To cheer my fellows on Life's road,
Who toil beneath their heavy load,

To share their burdens, smooth their way
By kindly words and deeds each day,
He bids me smile despite the rain,
And sing with joy Life's glad refrain.

God gave to me a few brief years,
A pathway fraught with doubts and fears,
Of sun and shadows, winds that blow,
That through my trials I might grow
In grace and wisdom, as each day
I journey on my toilsome way.

Rexburg, Idaho.   SARAH A. NELSON.

MESSAGES FROM THE MISSIONS

Prospects in the Netherlands Encouraging

The fifth semi-annual conference held at Utrecht, Netherlands, November 26-28, was very successful. The elders had a meeting on Thursday, November 25, and enjoyed their Thanksgiving feasts, both temporal and spiritual. The following days the public meetings were of note because of the large number of non-members who attended. Members, officers and teachers, as well as missionaries, enjoyed the meetings very much. Several have been baptized, and the prospects are encouraging.—*W. Gordon Rose,* conference president.

ELDERS OF UTRECHT CONFERENCE

Back row, left to right: Francis H. Gunnell, J. B. Bernards, S. B. Woolley, L. L. Bishop, Fred W. Newbold, R. Dale Snow, J. Herbert Milburn, W. M. Chipman. Front row: Reed M. Black, J. H. Dijkstra, Mission President John P. Lillywhite, Conference President W. Gordon Rose, Ray J. Hutchinson, Dan Simmons.

Latter-day Saints in South America

From Elder Waldo I. Stoddard, of the Church of Jesus Christ of Latter-day Saints in the South American mission, Buenos Aires, Argentina, Rivadavia 8968-70-72, we have received these interesting pictures, recently taken, of their two Sunday schools. Considering the recent organization of the mission, we are ready to state that they have a splendid start for a community of Latter-day Saints that will be felt for good, as time rolls on, in all that land. Elder Stoddard remarks that he has enjoyed the mission news of the *Improvement Era* from time to time, and modestly asks that the South American mission for the first time be also represented. We doubt that any mission can report a better showing, when the length of time since its organization is considered. From the looks of the youngsters, one would think that there is splendid material in Buenos Aires for an M. I. A. organization. Here's wishing that you may join us.

MEMBERS OF THE L. D. S. CHURCH IN SOUTH AMERICA

Six Baptisms in Gothenburg, Sweden

In October, six new members were baptized into the Church in this conference of the Swedish mission, making a total of nine so far this year in the conference. The members in the branch are faithful and a source of help to us in proclaiming the gospel. We find a large percentage of the people are inclined to treat religion with indifference and consider it a minor issue in life. We meet up also with many who are, as they call it, saved; but, in conversing with them, we find them quite ignorant of the principles of the gospel, with a lack of a knowledge of the real meaning of the scriptures and their message to the children of men. Through the inspiration of the Lord, we have been able to enlighten some who were in the dark concerning the new revelation of the gospel in the latter days. The elders laboring in this branch are: Emil G. Thedell, Park City, Utah; David H. Larson, Long Beach, California; Franklin S. Forsberg, Salt Lake City; M. Foss Smith, Snowflake, Arizona; and Erich W. Larson, conference president, Ogden, Utah.

Elder David O. McKay in Virginia

On November 20 and 21, Elder David O. McKay, of the Council of the Twelve, and President Charles A. Callis, of the Southern States mission, began the fall gatherings of that mission by holding a conference with the elders and Saints of Virginia, at Richmond. The attendance was good, all parts of the state being well represented. Valuable instructions and counsel were given by Elder McKay and President Callis. The past year has been a notable one. in this conference, new records having been made in baptisms and other lines of missionary activities. We are ever striving to become more efficient in our work, through humility and greater endeavor. We feel the old spirit of prejudice towards the gospel broken down. A greater desire on the part of the Saints to live the gospel is also noticeable. The *Era* is a great help to us.—*Arthur Peterson,* president Virginia conference, Richmond, Virginia.

ELDERS OF VIRGINIA CONFERENCE, SOUTHERN STATES MISSION

Front row, left to right: J. E. Eldredge, Woods Cross, Utah; A. L. Mortenson. Webb, Arizona; Charles A. Callis; David O. McKay; Arthur Peterson, conference president, Pocatello, Idaho; Philo V. Carter, Manassa, Colorado; A. H. Talbot, Panguitch, Utah. Second row: M. P. Christensen, Tremonton, Utah; T. H. Merrill, Salt Lake City; F. R. Epperson, Panaca, Nevada; O. Perkes, Hyde Park, Utah; K. E. Rosenlof, St. Anthony, Idaho; L. J. Foote, Gunnison, Utah. Third row: L. Horrocks, Neola; C. L. Karren, Lewiston; G. R. Hurst, Blanding, Utah; G. W. Fuller, Pine, Arizona. Fourth row: Wm. Behle, Jr,. Thatcher, Idaho; J. C. Spencer, Escalante, Utah; H. A. Faught, Taylor, Arizona; D. M. Shupe, North Ogden, Utah.

Success in the Rural Districts

We achieved splendid success in 1926, and the elders of the Norwich conference began the new year with the aim and desire to set the standards for 1927 a little higher. During the year 1926 special attention was devoted to missionary work in the country and rural districts, and thousands of the more humble folk listened to the message of the restored gospel. Frequently the elders received money and food to help them on their way. Six new fields were established, and many new homes are now opened to the elders; in addition, 115 separate towns and villages were completely canvassed from door to door; 65,000 tracts were distributed, 4,500 pamphlets, with a noticeable increase in the sales of the Book of Mormon and other books. Considerable interest is being shown by the people of the city of Peterborough, where eight of our Latter-day Saint brethren from Utah and Idaho, including Brother Thomas R. Cutler, who held the position of traveling engineer for the Utah-Idaho Sugar Company, and who is now engaged with Bishop Lewis W. Drake, from Burley, Idaho, and the others, by a British sugar company in connection with efforts to establish the sugar industry in England. It is with pleasurable anticipation and keen interest that we look forward to the reception of the *Improvement Era* each month, and we wish to thank those responsible for it.

ELDERS OF THE NORWICH CONFERENCE, ENGLAND

Sitting, left to right: Andrew E. Stewart, Sugar City, Idaho; Grant M. Broadhead, Beazer, Alberta, Canada; Leland N. Wight, outgoing conference president, Brigham City; William G. Bennett, conference clerk, Beazer, Alberta, Canada. Standing: Morgan Hawkes, Pocatello, Idaho; William J. Attridge, Rigby, Idaho; Clemuel J. Neville, incoming conference president, Rexburg, Idaho; Raymond Murphy, Salt Lake City.

Fifty-two Baptisms in Nine Months in Berlin, Germany

We are meeting with success in the capital city of Germany. During the first nine months of 1926, fifty-two baptisms were performed, and the regular services held in the eight branches of the conference were well attended by friends and investigators. In our regularly organized branches all the priesthood and auxiliary organizations are functioning, with the Saints, friends and missionaries all working harmoniously together for the forwarding of the work of the Lord in this foreign land. The *Improvement Era* is a great help in our work here. At our late conference a pageant was presented by the combined Sunday schools of the conference, entitled "Das Faterunser," and the work of the combined Berliner choir of a hundred voices, which sang several selections.—*Eulon Biddulph.*

Local Elders Conduct Bordertown Branch, Australia

This branch is two hundred miles from the main Adelaide conference, and is conducted by local elders, Stephen and Arnold Threadgold. They have a Sunday school organized, and faith-promoting services are held. Through the exemplary lives of the Saints, many are seeking to know more about the gospel and its fruits. A visit was made to the Bordertown branch of the South Australia conference by Elders Francis and Nelson, and they found the Saints energetic in explaining the gospel and in the execution of their duties. They were invited to the homes of quite a large number of earnest seekers after the truth, and many erroneous ideas were supplanted by the messages which they left. The work is advancing with pleasurable success. We enjoy the faith-promoting articles contained in the *Era,* and rejoice in the reports made by the various missions.—*Richard R. Francis.* conference president, Adelaide, South Australia.

MEMBERS OF BORDERTOWN BRANCH, SOUTH AUSTRALIA

Front row, left to right: Harold and Kenneth Threadgold. Middle row: E. Nelson, Howell, Utah; Arnold Threadgold; Richard R. Francis, Morgan, Utah, president of South Australia conference; Stephen Threadgold; Marjorie Threadgold. Back row: Maurice Lee Thomas, Rosa Threadgold, Thos. Virgin, Vera Threadgold, Ellen Virgin, Theo. Threadgold.

President Talmage Visits Austria

President James E. Talmage of the European mission, visited the Vienna conference, which embraces all of Austria. He was accompanied by President and Sister Hyrum W. Valentine of the German-Austrian mission, who had recently arrived to take charge of the work. They stopped in

Prague, Checho-Slovakia, enroute, and held a meeting in their hotel rooms with the Saints of that city.   A very inspiring missionary meeting was held the day following their arrival in Vienna, all the missionaries of the conference being present.   Conference was held on Sunday, November 28, 1926, all the sessions of which were indeed spiritual feasts, and were well attended by both members and friends.   Due, perhaps, to its distant location, only one other apostle (1897) ever visited this conference, and the people were thrilled with President Talmage's inspiring message, cheerful spirit, and his ability to speak a few words in their native tongue.   President and Sister Valentine were also well received and readily won the love and confidence of both Saints and missionaries.   After a short rest in Vienna, these mission officials, together with the conference president, visited the Saints in Northern Austria, and organized a new branch in Salzburg.   We are reaping good results from the visit of President Talmage and President and Sister Valentine; we have been able to make many new friends, and the work is progressing steadily.—*Eugene F. Pratt.*

MISSIONARIES OF THE VIENNA CONFERENCE, AUSTRIA

Sitting, left to right: Ralph W. Ford, Centerville, Utah, branch president at Linz; Hyrum W. Valentine, president German-Austrian mission; Ellen B. Valentine, president mission Relief Societies; Demoivre R. Skidmore, Brigham City, Utah, president Vienna conference; James E. Talmage, president European mission.   Standing: Clark T. Robinson, Beaver, Utah; Eugene F. Pratt, Arco, Idaho; Clarence A. Kirkham, Provo, Utah, president Vienna branch; Thomas Biesinger, Salt Lake City, 82 years old, 4th mission; Harold G. Hancock, Salt Lake City, Utah.

Inspiring Conference in Hannover

The Hannover district of the Swiss-German mission held a conference on the 14th and 15th of November.   President James E. Talmage, of Liverpool; President Fred Tadje of the German-Austrian mission, recently released, accompanied by his successor, President Hyrum W. Valentine, were present; also our own president, Hugh J. Cannon, with several conference presidents.   This was considered the most inspiring conference that had ever gone on record in the district of Hannover.   The Sunday meeting of the conference had an attendance of 272 in the afternoon and 375 in the evening. An outstanding feature of the meetings was a splendid pageant depicting "The Ideal 'Mormon' Home," presented by the Hannover Sunday school. The combined choirs of Hannover assisted. President Talmage spoke on the difference between "homes" and "houses." At the afternoon meeting the presidents bore strong and inspiring testimonies of the gospel and of the divinity of "Mormonism." Special sessions were held for the missionaries, who received valuable instructions from President Talmage and the visiting presidents. A Relief Society festival was enjoyed in Brunswick, following the conference, and all the missionaries gathered at Hannover to celebrate Thanksgiving in really American style. A good, hard game of football was, fought between two divisions of the missionaries, after which a savory banquet was given in our local hall to thirty-two missionaries. Sixty-one baptisms have been performed within the last year, and at the close of conference nine others were baptized at Hannover.—*Norman C. Pierce.*

The Canadian Mission

The year 1926 was a very successful year in missionary activities. During the summer a great deal of country work was done, and many people who had not heard the gospel received the message. Our prospects for the New Year are better than ever before. Our missionary force has been small, but we are receiving many new missionaries, and hope, through visits and meetings, to reap a rich harvest before the winter is over.—*Otis Orchard,* mission secretary.

MISSIONARIES OF THE NOVA SCOTIA CONFERENCE

Front row, left to right: A. Frelen Dahl, Raymond, Alberta, Canada, conference president; Joseph Quinney, Jr., Logan, Utah, mission president; Henry Rasmussen, Fairview, Utah, conference president, released. Back row: J. Willard Matthews, Panaca, Arizona; Leslie T. Maw, Ogden, Utah.

Twenty-three Baptisms in Texas

On November 5 the missionaries of the South and West Texas conferences met at Houston. Elder George F. Richards, of the Council of the Twelve, and Mission President S. O. Bennion were in attendance, and at the evening meeting spoke to a large audience, some of whom had traveled from distant sections of the state, making a special effort to be present. Many of the investigators present were greatly impressed with President Richard's remarks. President Vance of the West Texas conference reported fifteen baptisms; and South Texas, eight, in the past three months.—*John C. Sandberg, South Texas.*

· MISSIONARIES OF SOUTH AND WEST TEXAS CONFERENCES

Front row, left to right: D. C. Dana, Mexican mission; N. A. Durst, local; John C. Sandberg, president South Texas conference; S. O. Bennion, mission president; Geo. F. Richards, of the Council of the Twelve; Reed Vance, president West Texas conference; A. W. Steiner. Second row: L. F. Livingston; L. J. Bjorklund, O. W. Call, Mexican mission; Eugenia Vawdrey; Harriet Larkin; Norma Smith; Geo. V. Stewart; L. A. Larson; G. H. Williams. Back row: D. A. Alder, D. O. Bigelow, M. T. Marsh, L. Jensen, R. V. Liljenquist, D. S. Hymas.

Local People Help the Work Along

George H. Blunck, conference secretary, Zurich, Switzerland, furnishes an account of a Sunday School convention held there on the 3rd of October, at which time the superintendents of different branches of three conferences of Switzerland met with the superintendents of the Swiss Sunday schools and the missionaries and Mission President Hugh J. Cannon. It was the first meeting of its kind ever held in the mission and proved very successful. We were especially pleased to see the local people take such an interest in helping the work along. We have exceptionally good success in using the local people in our organizations, giving the missionaries more time to work with those who have not heard the gospel. The Zurich conference is presided over by a local man, as also are all of the branches except one. All these officers are punctual and up in the work and willing to do whatever may be required of them. Zurich is our largest branch, with about 225 members. We have baptized, so far this year, fifteen persons, a very good record, considering the condition existing in Switzerland at the present. We appreciate the *Era* very much in our work; it has surely been a great help to us.—*George H. Blunck*, conference secretary, Zurich, Switzerland.

ELDERS, S. S. SUPERINTENDENTS, AND PRIESTHOOD CLASS,
ZURICH BRANCH

Top: Back row, left to right: Blaine Bachman, president Bern conference.
George H. Blunck, secretary Zurich conference; L. D. Zollinger, Bern, released;
Elder Chamberlain, Bern; J. W. Stucki, Zurich. Second row: Waldo R. Frandsen,
St. Gallen; Earl J. Rhees, Luzern; Clinton M. Dinwoodey, mission secretary, Basel.
Third row: A. A. Hoffman, Zurich; Walter Trauffer, Zurich; J. Hamilton
Caldar, mission bookkeeper, Basel; Elder Sohn, editor *Stern*, Basel; Elder Kohler,
Bern; Dean W. Tucker, Zurich. Front row: Don P. Nebeker, St. Gallen, branch
president; Walter Ruf, Luzern; K. Ed. Holman, president Zurich conference;
Hugh J. Cannon, mission president; Elder Rinderknecht, Cologne, released; Elder
Weidmann, Bern; Lamont E. Tueller, president Bern branch.
Center: The Sunday School superintendents who came together at the convention.
Bottom: The Priesthood class of the Zurich Branch.

Elder George F. Richards in Oklahoma

At the regular quarterly conference held at Tulsa, Oklahoma, Central
States mission, Elder George F. Richards, of the Council of the Twelve, met
with the elders, giving them substantial counsel and very valuable sermons.
In the past three months we gained considerably over the previous three
months. Nine elders sold 107 Books of Mormon, 894 other books, held
193 meetings, and baptized seven persons into the fold of Christ. We
rejoice in the opportunity granted us in being called as ministers of the
gospel of truth. We all enjoy the monthly visits of the *Era*, and find
great comfort in its messages.—*Daniel K. Brown*, president Oklahoma conference, Central States mission.

Two Mutuals in Sheffield

Raymond H. Haight, Nether Edge, Sheffield, England, reports that the
traveling elders of that conference celebrated Thanksgiving day with a
genuine American dinner, at the home of Mr. and Mrs. Tow, who made
them very welcome. There are four branches of the Church in the conference,
with three fully organized Sunday schools and two organized Mutuals, one
M Men class and one Bee-Hive class. "The elders are having fair success
and we expect to baptize three before Christmas."

Elders laboring in the Sheffield Conference are: Harold E. Brown, M. B. Langford, Nathaniel E. Parry, Fred L. Finlinson, Raymond H. Haight, conference president; Clinton L. Mills, clerk; J. Deloy Hansen, James S. Chadwick, Eugene
H. Hall.

Many Friends Found

President Albert K. Bramwell, Peoria, Illinois, reports the elders
throughout that conference diligently at work, with the result that many
friends and investigators have been found, and additional cottage meetings
are held in homes during the winter. Through the courtesy of a certain
minister in Bloomington, the elders have permission to preach on Thursday
evening at a social mission church, and much good in proclaiming the gospel
should result from this opportunity.

The elders of the Northern Illinois conference are: Alton F. Jones, Hooper, Utah;
J. Mylo Wright, Delhi, California; Louis C. Larch, Idaho Falls, Idaho; James R.
Atkinson, Woods Cross, Utah, former conference president; Albert K. Bramwell,
Ogden, Utah, conference president; Gerald Frank, Alberta, Canada; Alma Heinle,
Huntington Park, California; Lyman Call, Woods Cross, Utah; Dewane M. Kelly,
Safford, Arizona; Leonard Peterson, Brigham City, Utah.

OUTSTANDING NEEDS

Of the Young Men and Young Women of the Church, and Some Proposed Ways of Meeting These Needs

(Compiled from suggestions volunteered by Stake and Ward M. I. A. officers, at the June Convention, 1926, edited by a joint committee of the General Boards; A. L. Beeley, chairman, Mary C. Kimball, and Ephraim E. Ericksen. It is recommended that the following be considered at the February meeting of Stake Boards, and that their findings be forwarded to the General Boards.)

I. RELIGIOUS.

    A. The Needs.

        1. Greater faith in God, and a stronger testimony of the Gospel of Jesus Christ.

        2. More active participation in and responsibility for Church and community work. Greater regard for the Sabbath day.

        3. Greater reverence for our religious leaders and our religious institutions.

    B. Proposed ways of meeting these needs.

        1. More adequate leadership. Specifically:

            a. Adopt the "one man—one job" policy.

            b. Make use of a larger number of individuals as leaders and use them in more specialized ways.

            c. Select leaders with natural aptitudes for dealing with the young people.

            d. Secure leaders who have a testimony of the Gospel, and as far as possible, possess a genuine spirituality.

            e. Prune the organization of its "dead timber" (i. e., amongst the officers.)

            f. Encourage M. I. A. leaders to attend sacrament meetings.

            g. Formulate a general policy and adopt a specific program for raising the training standards of M. I. A. recreational workers by means of:

                (a)   Leadership Institutes,

                (b)   Training Courses,

                (c)   Union Meetings,

                (d)   Fall Conventions.

            h. Encourage M. I. A. teachers and leaders to attend teacher-training classes.

            i. Stimulate teachers to painstaking, prayerful preparation.

            j. Enjoin teachers to avoid all forms of dogmatism. Arguments for and against a proposition should be analyzed and wherever possible facts and explanations furnished.

            k. Encourage leaders to read and apply the instructions contained in the *Journal* and the *Era*.

            l. Select and train M. I. A. leaders to provide individualized guidance and companionship to boys and girls. Encourage leaders to conversation with young people.

        2. Adopt more spirituality in the M. I. A. program.

        3. Hold up the ideal of the mission as a spiritual objective for all young people.

4. Encourage young people to go to the temples—especially for marriage.
5. Correlate the work of the M. I. A. with the work of the Priesthood.
6. Cooperate with the Bishopric in providing more interesting sacrament meetings. Feature the testimonies of young men and women on regular and special Fast days. Provide a full, stimulating program for the Sabbath day.
7. Give young people more opportunities to pray in public.
8. Conduct a campaign to make the standard Church works available in every Latter-day Saint home. Encourage the habit of scripture reading.
9. Stimulate the use of appropriate music as a means of inducing religious attitudes.
10. Make prayer a delightful and an integral part of our worship and procedure in all group recreational activities. Encourage family prayer.
11. Tell the story of old and new leaders in new ways.
12. Outline a series of renovation projects for our Church buildings in which M Men and Gleaner Girls can take responsibility. (e. g. landscape architecture, boys; interior decoration, girls.).
13. Encourage competitive essay writing on the various aspects of "Mormonism."
14. Provide opportunity by means of group discussion, play production, etc., for the study of other peoples, other religions, and other cultures.
15. Make a survey of all potential M. I. A. young men and young women in the ward; inventory their talents and aptitudes, and note their spiritual needs.

II. MORAL.

A. The Needs.
1. Greater dependability.
2. Higher standards of morality.
3. Greater modesty, courtesy, and chivalry.
4. Greater sympathy and brotherly love for other persons and other groups.
5. More definite life objectives and life ideals, and greater persistence in their pursuit.
6. Greater obedience to the Word of Wisdom.

B. Proposed ways of meeting these needs.
1. Teach the scientific soundness of the Word of Wisdom. Labor individually with those who are not keeping the Word of Wisdom.
2. Encourage dependability by making dependable persons, and dependable behavior prominent in the association.
3. Study the problems of dress systematically by means of:
   (a) Essay writing,
   (b) Lectures,
   (c) Demonstrations,
   (d) Dress reviews, etc.
4. Discuss at appropriate times and in appropriate places the spiritual aspects of such things as courtship, business, politics, etc.
5. Provide a short, practical course in the nature and evolution of morals.
6. Feature demonstrations of etiquette, etc., in connection with M Men's and Gleaner Girls' banquets, dances, etc.
7. Carefully select medical and educational experts to give talks about life and its sacredness.

8. Encourage parents to teach their children morality and the laws of physical growth.
9. Cooperate with the home and the public official in enforcing anti-liquor, and other important laws.
10. Keep the ideals and standards of Scout work and Bee-Hive work constantly before all young people.
11. In order to develop chivalry among young men, outline a series of projects—similar to those of Scouting, but of a more mature sort.
12. Encourage young people to make their own way in life without depending entirely upon their parents for financial help.
13. Encourage good movies—discourage unwholesome ones.

III. SOCIAL, INTELLECTUAL, AND OTHER NEEDS.

A. The Needs.
   1. More companionship between children and parents.
   2. Greater harmony in family relationships.
   3. A wider range of intellectual and physical interests in the recreational program.
   4. A greater interest in the fine arts.
   5. The spiritualization of secular interests.
   6. A clearer conception of the vital problems of life.
   7. A better understanding of young people by their elders.
B. Proposed ways of meeting these needs.
   1. Provide for more participation of parents in the recreational activities of their children.
   2. Stimulate greater companionship between parents and children by means of Fathers and Sons', and Mothers and Daughters' outings. Encourage home parties and home-evening programs.
   3. Organize hosts' and hostesses' committees as a means of supervising the social activities of young people.
   4. Employ intelligent and dignified means of advertising M. I. A. ideals and work.
   5. Provide for a wider range of self-directed activities after the order of M Men's and Gleaner Girls' work.
   6. Encourage the weekly half-holiday idea, and discourage social functions that continue late Saturday evenings.
   7. Multiply the opportunities to get young people before the public.
   8. Bring about a closer cooperation between the work of the M Men and the Gleaner Girls.
   9. Provide more competitive activities of all sorts.
  10. Stress dramatics and music.
  11. Arrange for fine arts programs on regular and special M. I. A. nights.
  12. Make a special effort to expand the traditional notion of recreation as merely physical activity to include the wider range of intellectual activities outlined in the *Recreational Bulletin*.
  13. Create or make use of a community organization of parents to consider the local needs of boys and girls. (For example, make this a project for the Advanced Senior Class, and devote one night a month to such discussion.)

Editors' Table

Who is to Blame?

Road houses are increasing unduly throughout the land. In Salt Lake county it has been found necessary to provide so-called strict regulations for them, especially regarding the attendance of the young people. They are to be excluded after nine o'clock, while the older people, perhaps their parents, are to be excluded at one o'clock the next morning; at least the outer doors are to be locked at that time. The vigilant supervisors, officers, directors and sponsors, some of them, perhaps, personally financially interested, are said to "stand ready to enforce existing laws and those to be made later."

It often happens that the youth of today are unjustly accused of a variety of faults by the older generation. It is not always the case that young people are going so far wrong as some of their immediate ancestors would have us believe. But if they do not, it is not because there is a lack of opportunities provided for them by their elders.

What children stand in need of today is early religious instruction in the home. Parents are too busy to give their children the fireside stories, the bed-time talks and instructions that the good teacher, Dr. Maeser, in his time, insisted were so necessary and desirable. The result is that children grow up with little training or instruction tending to belief in God and the works of righteousness. They become unwilling, as they grow up, to adopt the old standards of religion and ideals of character that have proved best through the ages, principally because their early training in this direction has been neglected.

There is lack of the old, splendid influences of the home life; in its stead there are the automobiles, movies, the modern dances, cheap theatres, the cabaret, cigarettes for men and women alike; and now and lately the road houses—fascinating doorways to iniquity. And the young people, without definite standards, are inclined to prove everything by trying it. They have spiritual longings, and seek to satisfy these longings for happiness in the vortex of material things, only to find in the end that these are inadequate. Why? Because one can not receive a fulness of spiritual joy through material sources. It must be coupled with faith, and the love of God, and be taught in the home, early, earnestly and persistently. The responsibility for such teaching, as so well stated in the Doctrine and Covenants (68:25, 28-31), is with the parents, and they are accountable for many of the slips and follies of youth. Parents must require their children to walk uprightly before the Lord, because they themselves are upright. They can not patronize road houses, and indulge in every modern extravagance and evil, and yet have influence with their children to do opposite. What is bad for youth is equally hurtful for those of mature years. The children revolt against hypocrisy; and, in search of better ways, themselves commit new follies—defy conventions, shock sensibilities, and in the process often do wicked things and inflict injury and cruel injustice upon themselves.

In the L. D. S. Church the youth are not entirely free from the doubts, evils and misgivings generally affecting the youth of the land. This is an indication that there are faults in their education and in the home training. On the whole, however, and that is an indication of correct training, our young men and young women are industrious, upright, straightforward, reasonable in thought and action, clean-minded, possessing high ideals and honesty without hypocrisy. They are young men and women who will not break their word of honor. They believe in God, have faith in the hereafter, and believe that, to insure real success in life, the spiritual and material must go hand in hand, both being necessary to their happiness and salvation. These are not engaged in the indulgence of excesses, nor found in the ways of the road house.

We are confident that the good judgment of the majority of parents, coupled with their example, wise teachings, tolerance and help, will guide the youth to right conduct and the love of God which is the beginning of wisdom. We believe also that our youth will have the moral courage to spend their leisure hours in such recreational activities as will result in good to them, and in potential values in their lives, in which case they will be sure to steer clear of the road-house, the cabaret and the night club.—A.

Reflections

Boost the Good—There is truth in the caustic statement, "Virtue is its own reward, but sin and iniquity get the advertising." If one does not believe that, let him look at the front page of his newspaper every day. If there is a wickedness or a vice or an iniquity committed, or if anyone has gone wrong, it is pictured there in large display. On the other hand, if there is anything virtuous or of good report, it is generally hidden on the inside pages among the advertisements, or never mentioned at all. In private life, we might well discard the newspaper style, and give virtue and good report a chance. For, notwithstanding all the advertising iniquity gets, there is more virtue than sin in the world. Give the good in a man a boost.

The Successful Teacher—The teacher who has the Spirit of God with him needs no signboards along the highway of life to tell of his virtues. A successful Advanced Senior class teacher in Southern Utah writes that the really successful teacher is the one who gets the greatest response from the members of his class. "That teacher gains most who has made the best preparation and who by tact transfers his preparation to others." We might add that conveying truth from the teacher to the student is a great science in itself and requires training; hence, our teacher-training classes.

Live Your Religion—The editorial policy of the *Improvement Era* is to urge every man to live up to the highest ideals of his religion. It is clearly a benefit to every man to do this, and to translate the high ideals of his religion into the actions of his daily life. The aim of the Y. M. M. I. A. is the policy of the *Improvement Era;* namely, "to assist every young man to complete living, on the foundation of faith in God and his great latter-day work."

Gaining Victory Over Evil—In and through ourselves, we are not capable of conquering the enemy of our souls. It is only when we receive strength from God to uphold our own efforts that victory over evil will be ours.

Constituents of Religion—Three things characterize religion: knowledge, emotion and action. Doing or acting is quite as important as knowing. Emotion is of little or no use without action. Religion implies right preparation, sympathy and performance.

English Becoming of Universal Usage

Dr. James E. Talmage, president of the European mission made an eleven-weeks' tour to different countries in Europe just before Christmas. In his report, he makes some enlivening remarks concerning language. We quote:

"Except in the line separating the German-Austrian and Swiss and German missions, the language of the people determines the boundaries of the missions.

"As to the many tongues in which people express themselves, much could be said. One is inclined to query whether this diversity of speech is to continue as long as the nations endure, or, whether some day mankind shall speak one and the same tongue. * * * Of all modern tongues, English is most generally prevalent as a foreign language, that is as the acquired speech of those to whom it is not the mother tongue. It is the well considered judgment of many to whom language is a specialty in study that English will continue to spread, until it shall become practically of universal usage, at least among the educated classes of all nations.

"But there are other languages than those spoken by lip and tongue. Thoughts may be given out, received and understood, between those who have no common speech. Particularly is this observable among the Latter-day Saints in different countries. They soon learn to understand the spirit and meaning of one who comes to them as a bearer of the gospel message, though he speak a foreign tongue.

"Another striking feature, amounting in fact to miracle and serving as conclusive testimony of the divine aid attending this latter-day marvel and wonder, is the relative facility with which our missionaries learn to speak the language of the people amongst whom they are appointed to minister. * * * In the course of the current journey, the writer has found elders who arrived in the field less than ten months ago, then utterly unlearned in the language to them foreign, now speaking freely and impressively in conversation and public discourse, and conducting classes in the auxiliaries, wherein the language of the country is used exclusively."

Priesthood Quorums

(All matters pertaining to the Aaronic Priesthood, presented under this heading, are prepared under direction of the Presiding Bishopric)

New Texts of Study Should be Adopted

Since the October conference, members of stake high councils appointed to look after the Aaronic Priesthood, together with bishops of wards, have been urged to have the quorums of the Priesthood fully organized and ready to begin the 1927 work on the first of the year.

One month of the year 1927 has now passed and we are somewhat disappointed in the number of orders received at the Deseret Book Company, for Aaronic Priesthood courses of study for the year 1927. This may be caused through the desire on the part of ward authorities to finish the 1926 work before taking up that provided for 1927.

Fearing that this condition exists, we take this opportunity to remind all interested in the work of the Aaronic Priesthood, especially parents who have boys who should be actively engaged in this work, that it is important that each Priest, Teacher, and Deacon should commence on the work provided, in order that the work outlined may be completed in time to take up the work which will be provided for 1928. Delays may prevent the completion of the work this year, causing some important work to be neglected or making it necessary to encroach upon the next year's work. Therefore, in order to promote uniformity in the lesson work of the Aaronic Priesthood generally the new lessons should be undertaken at once, even though the last year's courses may not have been completed.

We urge bishops and all concerned to secure the necessary outlines, which may be purchased at the Deseret Book Company for 10c each for the Teachers, and the Deacons, and 15c for the Priests, sent postpaid upon receipt of the money.

Central Park Ward Priesthood Attendance Contest

The Central Park ward of the Grant stake held a Priesthood attendance contest between the Melchizedek and Aaronic Priesthood members during the whole month of November. The losers were to banquet the winners, and the result was that the fathers furnished the banquet. The boys were very enthusiastic; and, in order to win, were successful in securing the attendance of adult members of the Lesser Priesthood. The result was that the bishop has since been able to ordain eight older men holding the Aaronic Priesthood to the office of Elder. The Grant stake Aaronic Priesthood committee, and the ward committee supervisors cooperated in promoting this contest. The average attendance during the month of November of the Aaronic Priesthood of the Central Park ward was 90% of the total enrollment, and this high average has continued during the months of December and January.

Changes in Officers

A change in the Morgan stake presidency was effected in December. George Sylvester Heiner was sustained as first counselor, and Edward H. Anderson, Jr., as second counselor in the stake presidency, and the latter released as high councilor.

In Cedar Third ward, Parowan stake, Walter K. Granger was appointed bishop of the new ward. Manila branch, Lyman stake, was changed to a ward, with Peter G. Wall, bishop, Manila, Utah.

A new mission president, Willard L. Smith, of the Samoan mission succeeded Ernest LeRoy Butler.

Mutual Work

Introductions to the M. I. A. Slogan—1926-27

February, 1927

"We stand for a testimony of the divine mission of Joseph Smith."

Monthly themes:

October—How to obtain a testimony.
November—The announcement of the restoration of the gospel.
December—The need of the restoration of the gospel.
January—The heavens are opened and the Lord speaks.
February—The Book of Mormon a testimony of the divine mission of Joseph Smith.

1. The bringing forth of the Book of Mormon (an abridged history of the ancient inhabitants of America) is a strong evidence of the divine mission of the Prophet Joseph Smith. This book is a message to the Lamanites, the American Indians, a remnant of the house of Israel, to the Jews and to the Gentiles. It was written by divine commandment and also by the spirit of prophecy and revelation, and contains the gospel of Jesus Christ in its fulness to the ancient inhabitants of this continent, and is a witness for the truth of the gospel of Jesus Christ and for the Bible. It is a revelation from God translated by Joseph Smith through the power of the Holy Ghost. It is a part of the divine mission of Joseph Smith.

2. When the angel Moroni visited Joseph Smith, he told Joseph that there was a book deposited, written upon gold plates, and giving an account of the former inhabitants of the continent and the source whence they sprang; and he also said that the fulness of the everlasting gospel was contained in it, as delivered by the Savior to the ancient inhabitants. For a brief analysis of the Book of Mormon and a short statement of its origin, read the enlightening account following the title page of the new edition of the Book of Mormon, 1920; and for the complete record, see Pearl of Great Price, pp. 43-57; and *History of the Church*, vol. 1, chapters 1 to 6, inclusive.

The angel Moroni, having shown the Prophet the place of the hidden plates, commanded him to go once each year to this hiding place, and the angel would be there to meet him and give him instruction and intelligence at each interview, respecting what the Lord was going to do, and how and in what manner his kingdom was to be conducted in the last days. Joseph went as he had been commanded. Finally, on the 22nd day of September 1827, the same heavenly messenger delivered them to the Prophet with this charge, in the words of Joseph, "That I should be responsible for them; that if I should let them go carelessly, through any neglect of mine, I should be cut off; but if I should use all my endeavors to preserve them until he, the messenger, should call for them, they should be protected."

In this manner the ancient record was brought forth from the earth as the voice of a people speaking from the dust. It was translated into our language by Joseph Smith, through the gift and power of God, and was part of the divine mission of Joseph Smith.

3. The promises of the Lord concerning the bringing forth of the book, and the blessings that shall come through it to those who shall bring forth the Zion of God at that day, and the testimony that shall come to the

Lamanites through it, are set forth in I Nephi 13:35-41.

Since this work was accomplished by the Prophet Joseph Smith, it is an additional evidence of his divine mission. The Book of Mormon establishes the truth of the Bible; it makes known the plain and precious things which were taken from that book; it makes known to all kindreds, tongues and people that the Lamb of God is the Son of the Eternal Father, the Savior of the world, and that all men must come unto him or they cannot be saved.

4. To any person who has received a knowledge of the Book of Mormon, and who has read it with a sincere heart, these instructions are given on how to obtain a testimony, as recorded in Moroni 10:4:

"I would exhort you that ye would ask God, the Eternal Father, in the name of Christ, if these things are not true; and if ye shall ask with a sincere heart and real intent, having faith in Christ, he will manifest the truth of it unto you by the power of the Holy Ghost."

It is through the power of the Holy Ghost that one may know the truth of all things, and, among them, that, "the Book of Mormon was preserved by angelic guardianship and brought forth by revelation and translated by what men regard as miraculous means." The sentiment quoted from the Book of Mormon is God's promise to men, "and His testimony must ever stand above and before the testimony of men." The translation of the Book of Mormon was part of Joseph Smith's divine mission.. (See Robert's *New Witness for God,* vol. 2; also the testimony of three witnesses and the testimony of eight witnesses, which are men's testimony to men.)

"And unto three shall they be shown by the power of God; wherefore they shall know of a surety that these things are true." (Ether 5:3.)

A Challenge

Superintendent Almon D. Brown and stake and ward officers of the Y. M. M. I. A. of the North Weber stake are deserving of special commendation for the splendid support that they have rendered this year, and in the past, to the *Improvement Era* and to the general fund. Three hundred and nineteen subscriptions, with cash accompanying, were handed into the office in October last, and by the 20th of December the stake had contributed $200 for the fund for the year 1927. Superintendent Brown gives as the reason for their success, thorough cooperation with the Church officers and a complete conversion of the officers of the Young Men's Mutual Improvement Association in the stake and wards. Superintendent Brown believes that as good work can be done in any and all the stakes of the Church, if officers are converted. He says they are not putting over these two special activities only, but are at the front with every other activity required of the association. When a requirement is put over at the proper time, it is not difficult to succeed. The stake stood well in the requirements on the Efficiency Report for December, and was headed trying for perfect in January. The stake officers hold conference from time to time with the officers of each ward, where the outstanding needs of the M. I. A. are discussed pro and con and conclusions reached for the benefit of all concerned. They are supported by the high council committee of two, who meet with the stake officers once a month to discuss the needs of the M. I. A. The stake board meet weekly. Attendance is marked for each member, also his attendance at Sacramental meetings. A report is handed to the stake presidency each three months, showing the service the board members are giving to the Church. The board members and officers are as willing to help the bishops in their work as they are to put the Mutual Improvement Association on its feet. Brother Brown writes, "We know that the other stakes have it over us when it comes to education; but when it comes to humility and work, and obedience to those in authority over us, and in the end success, we will make them sit up and take notice."

A Unique Meeting

New situations, of course, are very interesting. What was a new situation appeared in the Granite stake M. I. A. organization, on Tuesday evening, January 11, when all the ward organizations in the stake took automobiles to the stake house, and held a joint M. I. A. meeting of the associations. There were possibly more than two thousand young people in the Granite stake tabernacle to listen to the program, every seat and standing place being occupied. Appropriate songs introducing the slogan were sung. A young lady, Miss Whitbeck, gave a talk on the same topic, occupying probably six or seven minutes. At the close of her remarks, she stated that it was customary for the congregation to stand and repeat the slogan. Instead, owing to the large number present, she repeated it, "We stand for a testimony of the divine mission of Joseph Smith," and asked the congregation to bow their heads for just a moment, and prayerfully contemplate the statement, and ask for a testimony. As they were in this silent attitude, a chorus of young people, accompanied with beautiful organ music, sang a verse of the hymn, "An angel from on high." At the close of this very telling presentation, Elder Melvin J. Ballard, of the Council of the Twelve, occupied an hour and twenty minutes in a very effective talk, which as its basis gave the reasons why and the method how the young people should prepare themselves to prove worthy to receive the rich heritage which the Church and its organizations have prepared for them. It was an appeal to clean and righteous living; to think and act in harmony with the commandments of God. Elder Ballard's address was listened to with the closest attention, and at intervals complete silence prevailed. It was just such a spiritual feast as will greatly profit all who heard. Very appropriately, the large congregation joined with spirit in the closing song, "True to the faith."

Some Objectives in Reading the Book of Mormon

The following fourteen objectives in reading the Book of Mormon were given by Elder Kinkie, of the L. D. S. University, Salt Lake City, at a monthly union meeting of the officers of the M. I. A. in the Granite stake, and may be helpful to other officers and readers. He stated that no other book will create faith in the young people like the Book of Mormon:

Objectives:
1. A choice land above all other lands, chosen by the Lord. (Ether 13.)
2. The journey to the promised land. To whom was the land promised?
3. Records and plates.
4. Fulfilled prophecies. There are fifty-six fulfilled prophecies, at least, in the Book of Mormon.
5. Prophecies yet to be fulfilled. (III Nephi 20 and 21.)
6. Miracles, signs and wonders.
7. Movements and migrations of the peoples.
8. Gospel doctrines taught by the prophets.
9. Lands, cities, highways and animals.
10. Commotion and upheaval of the earth.
11. Christ's ministry among the Nephites. (III Nephi 11.)
12. Miscellaneous teachings—economics, etc.
13. Hiding up the plates, and final destruction of the Nephites.
14. The coming forth of the Book of Mormon, and the testimony of the two nations joining together. (II Nephi.)

What to do in February

The M. I. A. are suggesting for this season's work in drama:
1. A stake-wide contest in a one-act play;
2. The presentation of a standard drama.

We call attention, for information concerning the one-act play contest and the drama, to page 16 of the *M. I. A. Year-Round Recreation Program and Contests* for 1926-27. It is suggested that each ward put on three one-act plays, which would call a number of people into the activity and provide a full evening's entertainment. Extra programs may be obtained at the general office.

The Unequal Yoke, by Blanche Kendall McKey, the Jubilee prize play, published in the July *Improvement Era,* 1925, is one of the contest plays. The *Era* will also have a new play for the coming season, now ready to be published and which is intensely interesting. Eleven plays for this season are suggested in the *Recreation Program,* page 16.

Competent judges should be selected by the stake committee on Recreation to visit each ward. These judges will select, as a result of the ward production, three plays to come up for the grand stake finals. Much interest can be aroused for this big final stake night, at which time the stake prize winner will be selected. Rules for judgment are the same as the Church-wide drama contest, page 25 of the *Year Round Recreation Program,* in which nine plays are suggested to be used in case the one-act contest is not entered into.

Points to be remembered: Get 100% for January on Efficiency and Statistical Reports, and send into the general office by the 10th of February. Check on the study of the manuals. Ascertain how the contest in reading the Book of Mormon is going on in your ward and stake, and also the report on all the books of the reading course. See *Improvement Era,* page 198, for December. Why not determine in your ward to win the new reading course for 1927-28? Urge the Membership Committee to make plans for a continuation of a good attendance in your association till June.

M. I. A. Scout Work in Hamburg, Germany

The Boy Scout movement was inaugurated in the Hamburg, Germany, branches in January, 1926. It was hard to convert some of the old members to the new idea, but since they have learned to know the purpose and nature of the organization, the enthusiasm has waxed strong. The boys had just

GERMAN SCOUTS, HAMBURG.

been waiting for some opportunity to satisfy their inborn longing for outdoor life. The enrollment has steadily increased from the first day on, and now there are 55 boys enrolled. The accompanying pictures were taken in July.

The troops are now fully organized and equipped and have earned their own paraphernalia. Fests and entertainments, entirely arranged and led by the scouts, have been given and money has been raised to buy banners, staves, bugles, first-aid kits, tents, etc. A spirit of cooperation, not unlike that of the pioneers of Utah, prevails among these pioneers of scouting in this land. Money was provided by the group to buy material for uniforms for all and the sisters of the Relief Society made them. In all their undertakings the boys with more means help those with less, and no one has to stay home from trips on account of lack of money. The boys have displayed good business ability, and this little financial achievement of theirs is worthy of praise, considering the present depressed financial conditions of this country.

Many hikes have also been undertaken in the neighboring forests, and on one occasion the boys were separated in pairs and left upon their own resources to find their way at night to a city approximately 40 miles distant. Although the country was strange to them, they all arrived safely after "hoofing" it all night.

SCOUT MASTERS AND ASSISTANTS, HAMBURG, GERMANY

The boys are friends, and once they become Scouts, they become interested in the gospel and attend all the meetings, bringing their parents with them in many cases.

The future of the Scouts in this country is bright, and the time is not far distant when this organization will play an important part in spreading the gospel among the youth of this nation.—*Aaron C. Taylor.*

M. I. A. in the California Mission

Commencing October 4, and ending November 8, Elder Rulon A. Snow, president of Y. M. M. I. A. and superintendent of Sunday schools, and Sister Evelyn Schank, president of Y. L. M. I. A. and Primaries, together with Elder Jacob O. Gardner, mission secretary; Sister Dycie J. Law, corresponding secretary; Elder George H. Marchant and Sister Gerda Hendrickson, made an extended tour through Arizona and Southern California, in the interest of these organizations in the California mission. On November 11, President Snow was released to return home to St. George, Utah, and Elder George H. Marchant succeeded him, taking charge of the party on their tour through Northern California and Nevada. The Mutual work consisted of general instructions and discussion. All the young people were invited to attend, as well as officers and teachers. The Young Men and Young Ladies separated for their individual work. The mission officers and missionaries presented a musical program and one-act play. The program consisted of vocal solos, duets and trios, and piano solos and duets. *The Unequal Yoke*, the prize-winning play of the Jubilee year, 1925, was presented also. The program was given in a splendid manner and was greatly appreciated by all. Many investigators were in attendance and expressed appreciation and interest in the work accomplished by these young people. The M. I. A. work is progressing in a splendid manner; the young people are taking keen interest. and the officers and teachers throughout are putting forth every effort to place the M. I. A. in the California mission on a high level. The tour was completed December 15.—*Evelyn Schank.*

M. I. A. OFFICERS, CALIFORNIA MISSION

Front row, left to right: Gerda Hendrickson, pianist, Salt Lake City, (released); Evelyn Schank, president Y. L. M. I. A. and Primary, Salt Lake City; Dycie J. Law, corresponding secretary, Delta, Utah. Back row: Jacob O. Gardner, mission secretary, Afton, Wyoming; Geo. H. Marchant, superintendent mission Sunday schools and Y. M. M. I. A., Holliday, Utah.

Fremont Stake to the Front

We trust that it will encourage all the other stakes to know that Fremont stake, with 657 who should be enrolled, has an enrollment of 756, with an average attendance of 504, in fourteen wards, all of which reported; and ten points in every activity were made by the wards, and, of course, by the stake. That means that seventy-six, or 10% of the enrolled membership, or more, read twenty-five pages in the Book of Mormon during December. The average attendance in the Advanced Senior class was 151 out of an enrollment of 191. We congratulate Fremont stake upon its achievements in the activities of the M. I. A., and ask that the stake be not left alone in this achievement, but that many stakes will equal them. Quite a large number of them stood upon the brink in December, and were confident of going over completely in January.

M. I. A. Merry-Go-Round

The Shelley stake recently gave a splendid entertainment, under the direction of the stake boards, which was both a social and a financial success. Each of the nine wards of the stake were responsible for one part, not exceeding fifteen minutes time. The schedule worked out perfectly, and the program was carried smoothly, as the performers went from one ward to the next. The numbers consisted of one-act plays, aesthetic dancing, pantomimes, acrobatic features, folk-songs, a flower basket, short comedy skits, piano and vocal solos, etc. A cash prize of $15 and a second prize of $10 were awarded to the wards selling the greatest number of tickets according to the ward population. The Fifth ward won first prize, and the Taylor ward the second. The houses in each case were crowded to capacity. It has been decided, because of the success, to make it an annual affair. In case any of the stakes desire a copy of the program, we will gladly furnish the same. Wishing all a bigger and better M. I. A. for the coming year.— *Benj. B. Stringham*, stake secretary, Y. M. M. I. A., Shelley, Idaho.

M Men of Lund Ward hold Reunion

On December 22, 1926, the Third Annual Reunion of the M Men of the Lund ward, Idaho stake, was held at Lund. It went over big. Holiday colors decorated the hall and tables. Adhering to the custom of other years, the M Men brought partners, and sixty people sat down to the banquet, the main feature of the evening. Alexander I. Wilson, president of the M Men, delivered the welcoming speech. Humorous talks and debates were enjoyed, and jokes were prolific. Community singing and social dancing were enjoyed, before and after the banquet. President Wilson, master of ceremonies; Victor Frandsen, toastmaster; Henry W. Blauer, song leader. One former member and five honorary members were present. The organization is annually growing.—*Alexander I. Wilson, president.*

M Men and Gleaner Girls' Banquet

The M Men and Gleaner Girls' banquet was held at Mt. Pleasant, December 4, in the North Sanpete high school gymnasium. The Relief Society did the serving of the banquet, and 235 M Men and Gleaner Girls, together with officers, were served. The affair was in the charge of J. Seymour Jensen and A. W. Anderson, stake M Men and Gleaner Girls leaders, the latter acting as toastmaster. Each ward of the stake responded with a part on the program. Excellent music was furnished by the North Sanpete orchestra. Other numbers on the program were toasts, readings, songs, and a short address by Bishop John Wells of the Presiding Bishopric, who was attending the stake conference at the time. A most enjoyable time was had. A social dance followed the banquet, and the whole was a great success in every way.

Stake Board Change in Idaho Falls

. On January 9 the stake board of the Y. M. M. I. A., Idaho Falls, was reorganized. Superintendent Sylvan Olson and his counselors, Guy A. Poulsen and Reed Scott, and Secretary A. B. Wheeler, were released, and the following were sustained: Rolf C. Wold, superintendent; Ira J. Stoker and William Francis Burtenshaw, counselors; members of the board: Melvin Armstrong, chairman of stake Recreation Committee; John O. Mellor and J. W. West. The secretary will be selected at an early future date. The Y. L. M. I. A. stake board was reorganized at the same time with Sister Sarah S. Pond as stake president.

Current Events

A STUDY FOR THE M. I. A. ADVANCED SENIOR CLASSES
1926-27

(Prepared by the Advanced Senior Committee)

LESSONS FOR FEBRUARY, 1927

I—POLITICS AND INDUSTRY.

1.   Farm Relief.

One of the biggest questions before Congress in the present session will likely be the subject of farm relief. This question has been uppermost before the American people and Congress for the last year or two, and it does not appear as if there can possibly be any early solution to the problem. Each year the farmers are moving toward concerted action in order to push their own economic interests. The corn and cotton forces, for instance, have united in their demand for government relief. In the event that they should get it, it doubtless means that the surplus in the Treasury will not return to the tax payers. "Much will depend upon the form and scope of the farm relief measure," says the *Post*: "If it should include a proposal to revise the tariff downward it will meet with stubborn resistance. The legislators who firmly believe that the protective tariff is the backbone of all prosperity, including agriculture, will fight any proposal to reduce tariff." This 'means, of course, that the farmer cannot expect much tariff relief from them. There may be, however, efforts made in this Congress to try for both farm relief and tax relief, but the chances of success of either are quite remote. At least, if the tax payers are to benefit by the Treasury surplus it will be after a hot battle in Congress.

QUESTIONS

1. What are some of the most important questions before the agricultural interests in this country at the present time?

2. What is agricultural prosperity dependent upon after all?

3. Have the farmers in the past been inclined too much to the production of standard crops?

4. Should the farmers give their time to three or four specialty crops each year in order to avoid over production in some standard commodity?

5. If the farmers should resort to specialty crops, how would it affect the farmer who must buy wheat, corn, and cotton?

6. Is it likely that the agricultural interests will favor any tax relief unless they get farm relief?

7. What should this farm relief be composed of; that is, in what way can the government give the agricultural classes relief?

8. Should the government appoint a Federal Farm Board to study continuously agricultural conditions and ascertain where there is a surplus and what effect it has on prices?—See *Literary Digest*, December 18, 1926, page 8.

2.   The British Rubber Monopoly.

There is much talk of a credit "pool" which is about to be formed in the United States of $30,000,000 with which to buy crude rubber in the hope of stabilizing the price of that commodity, at least this is said to be the primary object of this "pool;" but by it they hope, also, to break the monopolistic grip of Great Britain on the rubber market. "This 'pool' plan," says the *New York World*, "was suggested by Secretary Hoover last year when rubber prices soared to $1.20 a pound. The present price is thirty-six cents a pound. Such a wide variation in the price of rubber has likely caused losses to many tire manufacturers." "But this buying 'pool' of our country," it is said by the *New York Evening Post,* "is a defense against, rather than an attack upon, the British rubber monopoly." "According to present plans about $30,000,000 worth of rubber will be purchased out of stocks in London, Singapore, New York, and the Dutch East Indies markets."

QUESTIONS

1. How will the American consumer and the American rubber and automobile manufacturer benefit by this combination?

2. What effect will it have upon the price of an automobile?

3. What causes competitive prices?

4. How far will the law of Supply and Demand and the cost of production apply in the price of rubber? of automobiles?

5. Will this pool stabilize prices, and if so, downward or upward?

6. Briefly, what are the motives behind this "pooling" of American resources and should it be taken seriously by producing interests?—See *Literary Digest,* December 18, 1926. page 12.

III. Utah and Her Resources.

"Considering all basic resources that contribute to the economic welfare of the race and the equally important natural wonders and scenic glories that yield the sources of geological history and stimulate the aspirations of heart and soul, the area marked by the boundaries of Utah is more richly endowed than any equal area that might be marked off on the surface of the globe," said President A. W. Ivins at a recent meeting before the Chamber of Commerce.

QUESTIONS

1. Is this statement of Utah's resources extravagant, and if not, why not?

2. What is the area and the population of Utah?

3. How does Utah compare in metal mining with other states in the Union? In silver? In copper? In lead?

4. How many square miles of workable coal has Utah? Of recoverable coal in tons?

5. In 1925 Utah broke the world record in the number of tons of tomatoes harvested per acre. She also produced one-half of the nation's alfalfa seed, and this year the yield from her farms equals nearly $100,000,000. In poultry, sheep, and cattle there has also been a great increase running into the millions, and her hay crop alone equals $13,500,000. Too, in scenic wonders and educational opportunities few states of the Union, if any, surpass Utah. Is it any wonder, therefore, that President Ivins made the above statement?—See Christmas edition of the *Deseret News* for 1925, and Section 6 for 1926.

II—SCIENCE

1. A bill is now before Congress to bring about the adoption of the metric system of weights and measures in the United States. The Senate Committee on Commerce has already conducted several hearings on the subject.

1. What is the metric system?

2. How does the metric system differ from the system of weights and measures now in vogue in most English-speaking countries?

3. What are the arguments for and against the proposed change?

4. Is it the business of the States or the Federal Government to legislate on such a matter? Why?—*Science,* December 31, 1926.

2.   At the recent International Conference on Bituminous Coal, held at Pittsburg, Pa., Dr. Frederich Bergius of Heidelberg, Germany, announced the results of long research in the extraction of gasoline and other valuable motor fuels, from low-grade coal.   Eminent authorities express the belief that the process of extraction "has passed beyond the experimental stage."

1.   How much coal is there in the world?

2.   Is the discovery of new oil resources keeping pace with the increasing consumption of gasoline?

3.   How much is known about the oil and coal resources of this Rocky Mountain region?

4.   What would be the effect of a sudden discovery of a new form of fuel oil?—*Literary Digest*, December 11, 1926.

3.   Indian graves yielding more than five hundred skeletons, and large quantities of pottery, weapons, ornaments, utensils, etc., have been discovered in a group of mounds known as "The Fisher Mounds" near Joliet, Illinois, by George Langford of that city.   Authorities regard this as "one of the outstanding archaeological developments of recent times in this country."

1.   What is archaeology?

2.   How does science determine the age of skeletons, weapons, pottery, etc., discovered in this way?

3.   How reliable are these scientific methods?

4.   Of what significance is such a discovery to Latter-day Saints?—*Science*. December 31, 1926.

4.   In search of the origin of cataracts on the human eye, Dr. John M. Wheeler of New York University Medical School took bits of living tissue from the eyes of embryo chicks.   These bits he placed in hollow-glass slides and kept them in incubators.   Every two days these detached tissue-cells reproduced themselves, proving, as Dr. Alexis Carrell of the Rockefeller Institute of Medicine has been doing for nearly fifteen years with his chicken-heart tissue, that "cell life can be maintained immortal apart from the parent body."

1.   How does research of this sort benefit humanity?

2.   Is it ethical for man to promote science and his own welfare by means of experimentation on animals?

3.   Who are the anti-vivisectionists, and upon what arguments does their case rest?

4.   Does Dr. Carrell's search for the physiological principle of eternal life seem justified religiously?—*Time*. January 3, 1927.

TEN OUTSTANDING MAGAZINE ARTICLES FOR DECEMBER, 1926

(Selected by a Council of Librarians)

1.   "Our Predicament Under the 18th Amendment." Walter Lippman, *Harper's*.
2.   "Love, Arms, Song and Death." Henry M. Robinson, *Century*.
3.   "The Book Collecting Game." A. Edward Newton, *Atlantic*.
4.   "The Man Behind *The Times*." Benjamin Stolberg, *Atlantic*.
5.   "Where Can I Find the Rules for Success?" Edward W. Bok. *Scribner's*
6.   "Portrait of an Olympian." Rollo W. Brown, *Harper's*.
7.   "Ringside Seats." Katerhine Fullerton Gerould, *Harper's*.
8.   "The Scientific City of the Future," Interview with Thomas A. Edison. *Forum*.
9.   "Americans Wanted." William S. Wasserman, *Atlantic*.
10.   "Phantoms of the Snow." Herbert R. Sass, *Good Housekeeping*.

III—RELIGIOUS AND SOCIAL MOVEMENTS

1. *Church Music.*

The committee on Church Music of the United Lutheran Church of America, which recently held its fifth semi-annual convention in Richmond, Virginia, condemns "show pieces" by the choir. The report says:

"All the choir's acts must he acts of worship, and if an anthem be sung, it must be chosen with due reference to the day, season or occasion, and be sung in a manner to inspire devotion." (See *Literary Digest*, November 20, 1926, page 37.)

Should the choir be regarded as a group of entertainers? What is the choir's place? What is the value of congregational singing? Is enough care given to fit the choir singing to the service? What may be done to have choirs and congregations sing with spirit and understanding?

2. *A Dearth of Intellectual Ministers.*

Dr. Henry Sloane Coffin, new president of Union Theological Seminary, New York City, claims that the church is not living up to its opportunity because of the mental deficiency of its ministers and "the unintelligible controversy over unimportant points." (See *Literary Digest*, November 27, 1926, page 31.)

Why is there such a dearth of intellectuals in the ministry? Does the condition of the religious world today show the need of preaching a Restored Gospel? What are requisites for one who would teach the gospel of Christ?

3. *What of Zionism?*

Dr. Henry S. Pritchett says, "The movement to colonize Palestine with Jews is unfortunate and visionary." (See *Literary Digest*, November 27, 1926, page 32.)

What has been said in refutation by those who favor Zionism? What do the Latter-day Saints think regarding the return of the Jews to Palestine?

4. *A Crisis in the Church of England.*

It is said that "A Supreme Crisis in the history of the Church of England is approaching, and some authorities think the day not far distant when it will become merged with the Church of Rome."—See *Literary Digest*, November 27, 1926, page 30.

In America, too, the Episcopal Church is astir over the growing power of the Catholic party within its ranks. *The Churchman* says, "Many intelligent laymen throughout the church are genuinely concerned, and not without cause. They see in the Catholic Congress a determined and organized effort toward a revival of magic and superstition in the church of their birth. They are beginning to fear the results of their own ignorance of what has been taking place. They have wished, and wish now, to be tolerant; but they are questioning whether under the plea of tolerance, they must sit idly by while primitive superstitions are promoted in the Episcopal Church by well-defined organization. They are coming reluctantly to recognize the truth of Bishop Randolph's statement that what we have in the Episcopal Church is not two schools of thought but two religions."—See *Literary Digest*, November 20, 1927, page 36.

What are the great differences in belief of the Roman Catholics and the Episcopalians?

What is common in the belief of the two churches?

What is the aim of the Anglo-Catholics?

Y. M. M. I. A. Statistical Report, December, 1926

STAKE	Should be Enrolled	No. Wards	No. Wards Reporting	Officers and Class Leaders' Enrollment	Ad. Senior Enrollment	Senior Enrollment	Ad. Junior Enrollment	Junior Enrollment	Total	Officers and Class Leaders' Attendance	Ad. Senior Attendance	Senior Attendance	Ad. Junior Attendance	Junior Attendance	Total
Alpine	1000	18	13	104	142	209	---	339	794	79	57	106	---	174	416
Bear River	480	12	10	81	127	90	49	93	440	58	97	66	19	79	319
Beaver	309	7	3	27	60	51	34	47	219	20	54	42	22	34	172
Benson	706	14	13	135	171	196	57	201	760	81	97	91	29	129	427
Box Elder	771	14	14	138	240	213	35	216	842	120	163	116	17	178	594
Cache	566	8	8	89	102	172	---	226	589	66	53	95	---	130	344
Carbon	590	10	4	31	20	34	8	45	138	27	36	28	---	43	134
Cottonwood	727	10	10	110	70	181	30	250	641	81	50	121	23	176	451
Deseret	493	12	12	102	160	104	20	155	541	71	94	60	15	90	330
Emery	476	9	8	56	46	141	---	154	397	45	23	83	---	131	282
Ensign	927	8	8	89	117	180	92	260	738	77	71	119	60	169	496
Garfield	308	8	4	33	36	22	---	30	121	22	28	17	---	16	83
Granite	1000	9	9	97	140	203	88	306	834	81	103	131	67	208	590
Grant	1400	14	14	129	109	310	59	357	964	107	99	226	26	233	691
Gunnison	279	7	7	50	73	68	25	68	284	40	50	28	14	60	192
Hyrum	500	10	6	52	82	85	20	74	313	34	50	51	18	50	203
Jordan	1011	16	8	68	83	135	64	230	580	53	49	93	39	152	386
Juab	337	5	5	39	74	73	---	120	306	39	37	40	---	54	170
Kanab	226	6	6	50	52	38	25	72	237	46	38	30	18	45	177
Liberty	1407	12	12	147	197	315	219	331	1209	116	100	164	139	235	754
Logan	597	11	7	74	60	116	12	197	459	56	27	65	9	104	261
Millard	344	8	6	48	64	59	---	76	247	42	48	40	---	67	197
Morgan	205	10	7	55	59	38	9	55	216	46	43	28	6	38	161
Nebo	454	9	8	69	78	90	4	213	454	60	50	50	---	150	310
North Davis	462	7	6	54	48	80	19	112	313	40	27	43	16	62	188
North Sanpete	700	10	9	73	59	170	20	176	498	54	36	92	13	118	313
North Sevier	275	6	6	40	62	65	---	57	224	32	35	37	---	40	144
North Weber	617	13	13	103	49	155	8	231	546	80	27	84	4	133	328
Ogden	848	10	10	99	144	231	65	250	789	72	60	133	43	148	456
Oquirrh	495	5	5	69	61	106	10	163	409	51	33	54	2	96	236
Palmyra	487	8	8	68	121	115	42	197	543	50	66	72	24	135	347
Parowan	532	10	10	67	141	82	10	89	389	48	75	46	12	63	244
Pioneer	785	10	10	101	98	215	15	233	562	72	44	115	4	111	346
Roosevelt	303	13	6	43	50	44	15	55	207	33	39	33	14	34	153
St. George	680	14	13	193	189	156	59	597	1194	70	99	114	15	105	403
Salt Lake	1072	13	13	143	137	225	134	238	877	105	75	130	71	156	537
San Juan	192	4	3	26	43	50	38	46	203	19	34	36	15	30	134
Sevier	353	6	6	54	77	120	54	105	410	38	40	73	34	73	258
South Davis	532	8	3	25	29	33	---	83	170	19	20	21	---	51	111
South Sevier	327	8	4	27	30	8	7	41	119	22	21	8	-7	27	85
Summit	467	12	7	45	47	64	9	52	217	28	17	40	9	29	123
Tintic	271	5	5	38	78	20	14	107	257	26	43	18	10	75	172
Tooele	390	10	5	46	53	44	27	51	221	30	26	22	15	23	116
Uintah	410	10	10	75	118	128	---	134	455	58	78	110	---	100	346
Utah	1100	16	12	118	128	235	24	262	767	78	89	152	22	182	523
Wasatch	382	9	7	60	84	90	---	124	358	47	46	53	---	92	238
Weber	711	9	9	78	70	120	48	173	489	60	39	70	18	109	296
Bannock	240	6	4	30	39	21	9	33	132	17	25	13	7	10	72
Bear Lake	363	11	11	95	79	113	---	141	428	59	67	84	---	80	290
Boise	365	10	8	---	---	---	---	---	329	---	---	---	---	---	296
Burley	305	9	4	34	65	24	17	44	184	28	49	18	14	35	144
Cassia	170	6	6	39	57	44	2	59	201	38	48	24	1	34	145
Curlew	124	10	6	39	56	27	---	53	175	22	22	14	---	29	87
Franklin	420	11	11	103	119	114	---	174	510	71	56	79	---	93	299
Fremont	657	14	14	161	191	167	31	206	756	87	151	110	21	135	504
Idaho	178	9	9	77	86	26	12	42	243	51	52	17	6	27	153
Idaho Falls	530	12	8	104	175	115	30	124	548	61	60	40	14	40	215
Lost River	69	3	3	20	46	14	---	37	117	15	23	3	---	16	57
Malad	305	7	6	63	79	69	11	90	312	50	49	38	---	61	198

STAKE	Should be Enrolled	No. Wards	No. Wards Reporting	Officers and Class Leaders' Enrollment	Ad. Senior Enrollment	Senior Enrollment	Ad. Junior Enrollment	Junior Enrollment	Total	Officers and Class Leaders'	Ad. Senior Attendance	Senior Attendance	Ad. Junior Attendance	Junior Attendance	Total
Minidoka	240	8	3	19	40	23	---	27	109	18	23	14	---	16	71
Montpelier	367	13	13	84	95	98	7	134	418	53	56	62	7	61	239
Oneida	370	11	10	92	100	73	8	148	421	64	50	42	6	96	258
Pocatello	561	10	10	102	102	119	24	166	513	70	65	71	28	95	329
Raft River	160	8	4	28	26	22	7	22	105	16	9	12	3	16	56
Rigby	521	13	10	116	146	87	38	98	485	80	120	52	25	59	336
Shelley	319	9	9	96	119	76	---	90	381	61	74	43	---	55	233
Twin Falls	210	5	4	24	62	34	---	57	177	15	22	20	---	34	91
Yellowstone	370	10	9	60	93	60	---	68	281	44	64	34	---	46	188
Big Horn	322	7	6	53	77	50	41	73	294	45	27	58	13	47	190
Juarez	128	5	5	27	68	26	27	55	203	22	60	22	23	47	174
Lethbridge	234	9	9	76	96	80	24	73	349	59	52	46	21	49	227
Los Angeles	526	16	13	108	138	241	15	119	621	78	90	162	8	80	418
Lyman	220	8	7	55	98	80	5	68	306	42	86	58	5	50	241
Maricopa	428	8	8	80	90	129	11	131	441	61	75	81	8	88	313
Moapa	237	9	8	65	88	92	10	96	351	38	43	67	6	75	229
Nevada	158	5	4	34	48	14	12	54	162	28	43	6	9	39	125
St. Joseph	214	16	6	56	58	59	29	77	279	39	23	36	17	39	154
San Luis	200	5	3	5	9	9	---	8	31	4	5	5	---	11	25
Snowflake	280	9	8	57	102	71	20	77	327	35	58	40	15	41	189
Star Valley	359	11	11	115	75	128	---	93	411	69	42	64	---	57	232
Taylor	344	6	6	67	88	125	73	47	400	55	71	90	51	31	308
Woodruff	335	6	5	39	71	64	7	63	244	34	37	24	5	36	136
Young	95	6	5	33	25	58	19	30	165	28	20	40	13	28	129
Calif. Mission	1046	34	29	174	314	213	24	155	880	137	213	155	5	115	625

Y. M. M. I. A. Efficiency Report, December, 1926

STAKE	Membership	Average Attendance	Recreation	Scout Work	M Men	Reading Book of Mormon	"Era"	Fund	Monthly Stake and Ward Officers' Mtgs.	Ward Officers' Meetings	Total
Alpine	8	5	7	7	7	4	10	6	10	9	73
Bear River	9	10	8	10	6	5	8	7	8	8	79
Beaver	7	10	8	7	8	5	5	8	8	7	73
Benson	10	6	9	9	6	4	7	7	8	9	75
Box Elder	10	10	10	8	8	8	9	9	10	10	92
Cache	10	6	9	10	10	6	10	8	10	9	88
Carbon	2	10	10	8	8	8	4	1	10	10	71
Cottonwood	9	10	10	10	10	5	6	6	10	9	85
Deseret	10	6	7	10	6	8	10	8	8	7	80
Emery	8	10	9	9	8	4	7	6	9	9	79
Ensign	8	10	10	10	10	9	10	6	10	10	93
Garfield	4	10	10	5	8	10	7	4	10	10	78
Granite	8	10	10	9	10	5	7	5	10	10	84
Grant	7	10	10	10	10	4	9	3	10	10	83
Gunnison	10	10	9	3	8	8	7	7	8	9	79
Hyrum	6	7	6	5	6	4	6	6	6	6	58
Jordan	6	10	5	5	5	3	4	3	5	5	51
Juab	9	6	10	6	10	9	9	7	10	8	84
Kanab	10	10	10	8	10	5	10	8	10	8	89
Liberty	9	6	10	10	10	9	9	10	10	10	93
Logan	8	6	10	10	10	6	7	7	10	10	84
Millard	7	10	8	5	7	2	5	4	8	7	63
Morgan	10	10	5	1	4	5	9	10	9	7	70
Nebo	10	7	7	4	6	3	6	6	8	9	66

STAKE	Membership	Average Attendance	Bon	Scout Work	M Mn	Reading Book of Mormon	"Era"	Fund	Monthly Stake and Ward Officers' Mtgs.	Ward Officers' Meetings	Total
North Davis	7	6	9	10	9	6	10	9	9	9	84
North Sanpete	7	6	8	10	8	5	9	6	5	6	70
North 'Sevier	8	7	10	8	7	2	3	6	5	6	62
North Weber	9	6	8	10	8	9	10	10	10	10	90
Ogden	9	6	10	10	9	8	10	9	10	10	91
Oquirrh	8	6	10	10	10	7	9	10	10	10	90
Palmyra	10	6	7	9	10	7	9	9	7	9	83
Parowan	7	6	8	6	8	5	6	5	6	8	65
Pioneer	8	5	9	7	10	5	8	6	10	10	78
Roosevelt	7	10	4	1	1	4	4	4	4	5	44
St. George	10	3	10	10	9	10	9	8	----	10	79
Salt Lake	8	6	10	10	10	6	7	10	6	10	83
San Juan	10	10	7	4	2	7	7	6	7	7	67
Sevier	10	6	7	7	6	4	10	9	10	10	79
South Davis	3	10	3	2	2	5	1	1	3	1	31
South Sevier	3	10	3	2	4	4	4	3	3	4	40
Summit	5	6	5	3	1	3	10	6	4	4	47
Tintic	10	10	10	10	4	8	8	3	8	10	81
Tooele	6	5	5	1	1	4	4	3	4	4	37
Uintah	10	10	10	3	8	10	8	7	10	8	84
Utah	7	10	9	9	10	5	8	6	10	10	84
Wasatch	9	10	6	6	7	4	6	7	7	6	68
Weber	7	6	10	10	10	6	5	4	10	10	78
Bannock	6	6	5	4	4	4	3	4	3	5	44
Bear Lake	10	10	7	5	7	7	10	8	8	8	82
Boise	9	9	9	2	6	8	7	4	9	9	72
Burley	5	10	4	4	2	3	3	3	4	4	42
Cassia	10	10	10	9	10	10	10	10	10	10	99
Curlew	10	5	7	----	1	5	10	10	6	4	58
Franklin	10	6	10	10	8	7	10	10	9	8	88
Fremont	10	10	10	10	10	10	10	10	10	10	100
Idaho	10	6	9	9	8	8	10	9	6	6	81
Idaho Falls	10	4	10	8	9	8	9	8	8	8	82
Lost River	10	5	10	7	7	5	10	5	8	10	77
Malad	10	6	7	10	9	7	10	10	10	10	89
Minidoka	5	10	10	3	10	7	7	7	10	8	77
Montpelier	10	5	7	4	5	6	8	8	5	8	66
Oneida	10	6	9	9	5	3	9	8	7	8	74
Pocatello	9	6	10	10	9	10	10	10	10	10	94
Raft River	6	5	7	----	1	2	4	8	5	6	44
Rigby	9	10	7	6	5	8	8	8	8	6	75
Shelley	10	6	10	9	5	7	9	8	7	8	79
Twin Falls	8	5	9	4	4	7	5	5	4	8	59
Yellowstone	8	10	10	2	3	6	9	9	7	8	72
Big Horn	9	6	9	5	4	6	6	8	6	8	67
Juarez	10	10	10	8	9	6	10	10	5	10	88
Lethbridge	10	10	7	10	9	10	10	10	10	10	96
Los Angeles	10	10	10	8	10	2	5	8	10	10	83
Lyman	10	10	8	7	6	5	8	7	4	6	71
Maricopa	10	10	10	10	10	10	10	9	10	10	99.
Moapa	10	7	9	6	7	7	8	8	8	6	76
Nevada	10	10	8	2	----	1	9	8	. .	8	56
St. Joseph	10	6	9	4	4	8	10	8	10	8	77
San Luis	2	10	10	10	----	10	10	10	10	10	82
Snowflake	10	6	6	5	6	2	7	5	4	6	57
Star Valley	10	6	9	5	6	7	8	8	5	9	73
Taylor	10	10	10	10	10	10	10	10	8	10	98
Woodruff	7	6	10	10	5	6	5	6	6	7	68
Young	10	10	10	----	4	8	7	4	8	8	69
Calif. Mission	8	10	9	4	5	6	7	8	10	9	76

Passing Events

Yoshihito, the emperor of Japan, died, Dec. 25, 1926, of an attack of bronchial pneumonia. Prince Regent Hirohito was immediately proclaimed emperor.

Fire in the Lourier Palace Movie theatre, at Montreal, Canada, took a toll of seventy-five lives, mostly little children, Jan. 9. The fire itself is described as trivial, but the fear-stricken Sunday audience jammed the exits, and many were suffocated. The fire seems to have started in a room under the balcony.

Solomon J. Salisbury, a nephew of the Prophet Joseph Smith, passed away at his farm near Carthage, Ill., according to a dispatch from that place dated Jan. 18, 1927. He was 91 years old. He is said to have been "a loyal 'Mormon'" until his death, although he did not join the Saints in Utah, owing to the opposition of his wife.

The seventeenth legislature of Utah convened Jan. 10, 1927, at noon. Alonzo B. Irvine, of Salt Lake, was reelected president of the senate, and Samuel M. Jorgensen, Salina, speaker of the house. The Catholic bishop, John J. Mitty, was invited to offer prayer. Chief Justice Samuel R. Thurman, of the supreme court administered the oath. In the house the members were sworn in by Justice James W. Cherry.

The automobile death-rate in Salt Lake City in 1925 was higher than in any other of the cities in the United States, except Camden, N. J., and Hartford, Conn. The percentage of persons killed here during the year, according to figures made public by the U. S. department of commerce, was 32.1 per 100,000. In Chicago the percentage was 21.5 per 100,000 and in New York 18. Denver had the lowest percentage with 13.2.

The recent Biennial Report of the Utah Agricultural Experiment Station is just off the press. It contains many problems of major importance both to the farmers and homemakers of the state. This report, known as Utah Experiment Station Bulletin No. 198, and prepared by Director William Peterson, covers the activities of the Station for the 18-month period from January 1, 1925, to July 1, 1926. Copies free at Logan, Utah.

Secretary of State Kellogg, on Jan. 12, in a statement to the foreign relations committee of the Senate, showed that the soviet leaders in Russia, according to their own public utterances, regarded Mexico and Central America as points of vantage, from which to assail the "imperialism" of the United States, and that the proceedings of communist conferences, both in Russia and the United States, proved revolutionary designs on this country.

The value of the crops of Utah for 1926 is estimated at $35,000,000. This is considerably less than the value of the crops for 1925, which was $50,000,000. But it is more than the total for 1924, which was only $33,000,000. The leading crop is hay, valued at $14,370,000. Wheat comes next, with $5,772,000. The potato crop is valued at $2,588,000. The sugar beets at $2,454,000, and the alfalfa seed at $2,338,000, which is about half of the yield for 1925.

State Senator LeRoy Dixon died, Dec. 28, 1926, at his home in Provo, following an illness of five weeks. At that time he was operated upon after the extraction of a tooth, but it was evident to the physicians that the end would soon come. He was born in Provo, Oct. 16, 1881, the son of Henry Aldous and Sarah DeGrey Dixon. He was elected to the state senate in 1922, and re-elected at the last election. In 1906-08 he labored in the British mission. He has served in the Provo city council six years, from 1911, and was then elected mayor twice.

President Coolidge sent a special message to congress, Jan. 10, 1926, explaining the government's policy in Nicaragua. He said he was acting in harmony with the declared policy of the Central American republics, not to recognize a government that has been established by revolutionary methods. That is the reason, he says, why we recognize president Diaz, and not the claims of Sacasa, who is in exile. That is also the reason why American marines have been landed, to prevent "outside" influence from interfering Besides, there are Americans residing in Nicaragua, who must be protected.

Henry W. Lunt, former state senator and member of the state road commission, died at his home in Cedar City, Utah, Dec. 26, after an illness that extended over several weeks. Mr. Lunt was born in Cedar City, Jan. 25, 1863, the son of Henry Lunt and Mary Ann Wilson Lunt, who had gone to Cedar City the year before to found that colony, the elder Lunt having been placed in charge of the colonization work there. As a boy and a young man he spent his life in the open, chiefly following the range, and many were the interesting stories he could tell of life in Utah in that era.

Robert W. Sloan passed away, Dec. 27, 1926, on his way to a hospital He had been ill for some time. On Christmas day he visited the graves at Logan of two sons, and the effort seemed to be too much for him. He came to this country from Ireland, when he was eight years old. He obtained employment at the *Salt Lake Herald,* when that paper was started, and remained in its employ for years. In 1889-90 he filled a mission for the Church in Great Britain. In 1897-8 he was a member of the legislature. About five years ago he went to San Francisco. He was widely known, affectionately, as "Bob" Sloan.

A severe earthquake was felt, Dec. 18, 1926, at Lisbon, Portugal. It was accompanied by subterranean noises. The waters of the Tagus river rose considerably and soon the surface was covered with thousands of fish. Cafes, theatres and business houses were hurriedly vacated. The facade of the central railway station was cracked from top to base. Trains were delayed several hours while a thorough examination was made of the tunnels. Another shock occurred at 6 o'clock next morning, many buildings being badly shaken. Two shocks were felt at Ventura, Cal., Dec. 19, at 1:05 and 2:45 a. m., respectively. No damage was reported.

The voice of the pope, Pius XI, was heard Dec. 20, 1926, in an address, or allocution, as they call it in Rome, before a "secret" consistory. According to the published accounts, the pontiff denounced in unmeasured terms the Mexican government on account of the "persecution" that has been "raging" there "with inhuman ferocity" for months. "We have been informed," his holiness said, "that venerable bishops have been torn from their sees, the government concentrating, incarcerating and even killing pious ecclesiastics and slaughtering the unarmed faithful praying before the venerated sanctuary of the most holy Virgin." And yet, president Calles is, as far as known, a member of the Catholic church.

Mr. Briand sends a Christmas message to the American press, in which he denies the truth of the old adage that the best way to preserve the peace is to prepare for war. He points out that France and Germany now, for the first time in history, are cooperating for the preservation of peace, and then adds: "Like Dr. Stresemann and Foreign Secretary Chamberlain, I am convinced that the year 1927 will see a new spirit and a new. conception of international affairs more widely spread through the minds of the peoples, and then there will be really something changed in the destinies of humanity. No other people can associate itself in mind and heart more earnestly in the realization of such a hope."

The school land question has, evidently, found its solution. The U. S. house of representatives, on Jan. 17, 1927, passed unanimously the bill, giving to the states all school sections, mineral as well as non-mineral. The bill bore the number and name of the Jones bill, which, in more general terms, had passed the senate last session. The house committee struck out all after the enacting clause of the Jones bill, substituted the language prepared by Secretary Work, and, by unanimous consent, the senate now can concur in the house amendment and the bill will be on its way to the president for signature. Senator Smoot thinks this procedure will be followed, and Senator Jones of New Mexico, author of the original bill, is entirely satisfied with the Work bill.

The 'Utah State Society of Long Beach, California, recently planted a tree in honor of President Brigham Young, at a flag celebration there. The Utah flag was carried by David Armstrong, a boy scout formerly of Salt Lake City, now of 260 Ausota Avenue, Long Beach. For the first time in the history of the nation, speakers said, forty colorful flags were unfurled to the breeze at the tree-planting exercises, held at Recreation Park, under the auspices of the Federation of States Society. There were flags from Wales, Scotland, Canada and France. Following the flag display eighty-five trees were set out in Federation Drive. Each tree represented either one of the presidents of the United States, or an illustrious deceased man or woman of the various states, territories and countries having societies in Long Beach affiliated with the federation.

David K. Udall, St. Johns, Arizona, former president of the stake, has been appointed president of the Arizona temple at Mesa, Arizona, the announcement being made by the First Presidency on Tuesday, Dec. 8. President Udall is one of the foremost pioneers of Northern Arizona, having taken a. prominent part in the development of that part of the state. President Udall was formerly of Nephi, and moved to Kanab in 1878, following a mission to England. In 1880 he was called by President John Taylor to become bishop of St. Johns, serving in that capacity for seven years, and following that was made president of the stake, in which office he served for thirty-five years, until the stake was reorganized in 1922, when he was ordained a patriarch. He was a member of the Twentieth Arizona Territorial Legislature and a member of the Highway Commission of that state, and for forty-five years has been engaged in carrying United States mails.

The sugar manufacturing business is in its early stages of development in Great Britain, where the climate and soil appear to be favorable for beet culture. Mr. Thomas R. Cutler, the engineer in charge, accompanied by seven others, residents of Utah and Idaho, among them Lewis W. Drake, Burley; Norman Drake, Burley; Claude W. Cawley and Frank Martin, Ogden; Archie Roberts, Hooper; Richard Young, Providence; and Henry Thomas, Lehi, have been engaged by the Central Sugar Company, Ltd., a British institution, to aid in the efforts to establish the sugar industry in England, where they are building a new sugar factory in Peterborough. These Americans, who, by the bye, are members of the Church of Jesus Christ of Latter-day Saints, have won the high esteem of the men laboring under them, and they have been employed because of their proficiency and the success of the industry in Utah and Idaho. Their methods will therefore be introduced in Great Britain.

President and Mrs. Heber J. Grant spent two weeks of January visiting in California. They went from Salt Lake to Cedar City, Utah, where they attended the funeral services for President Henry W. Lunt. From Cedar City, they went by automobile to Lund, and thence by train, in company with Mr. and Mrs. David P. Howells, to Los Angeles, remaining there a week. On January 2, President Grant attended the Sunday school in the Adams ward, and the services in the Huntington Park ward the same evening. The Sunday following, January 9, he was present at the conference meeting of the missionaries in the morning; in the afternoon he attended the services in the Home Gardens ward, and there dedicated a new meeting house; and in the evening dedicated a new meeting house in the Lankershim ward. The President spent some time visiting with friends and at golf, and returned home feeling well, after a most delightful trip. He reports a very encouraging and satisfactory growth in the Los Angeles stake and the California mission during the last year.

Ex-empress Marie Charlotte, widow of Maximilian, the ill-fated pretender who was killed in Mexico in 1867, died at Brussels, Jan. 19, 1927, of pneumonia, 86 years old. With her death, one of the most tragic characters makes her exit from the stage of history. She was married, when only 17 years of age, to Maximilian, the Austrian archduke, and they lived for a short time a most romantic life. Then, Napoleon III was induced, probably by papal influence, to invade Mexico in support of the clerical party, and Maximilian was induced to head the expedition and to proclaim himself emperor. His young wife, it is said, urged him on to this enterprise against the struggle for liberty in Mexico. But he lost out, and when Charlotte saw that the fatal end was approaching, she hastened to Europe and implored Napoleon, and other potentates, and finally the pope, not to abandon their tool in the hands of the Mexican liberals. But her appeals were all in vain. In fact, they were powerless to save the man whom they had helped on to destruction. And, finally, after her fruitless humiliation before the pope, she is said to have lost her reason, and was found wandering the streets of Rome, babbling incoherently. She has been tenderly cared for all these years, first by her brother Leopold II, and then by the present Belgian royal family. The tragic end of all concerned in the Maximilian invasion of Mexico is a striking testimony to the truth of the prophetic utterance in the Book of Mormon, which positively states, that "he that raiseth up a king against me shall perish," (2 Nephi 10:14.) That is just what Napoleon's attempt in Mexico was. It was an effort against liberty and in favor of despotism, particularly clerical. Napoleon was captured by the Germans, Sept. 1, 1870, and died in exile. Maximilian was killed by his enemies, abandoned by his "friends," June 19, 1867, and his wife lost her reason. Bazaine, with 170,000 men, 6,000 officers and 3 marshals, surrendered Metz to the Germans, for which in 1873 he was sentenced to death as a traitor, the sentence, however, being commuted to imprisonment. He fled to Spain and died in exile. As for Pius IX, he lost every vestige of political power when the Sardinians occupied Rome in 1870, and caused his holiness to consider himself a captive in the Vatican.

"I AM NOT RELIGIOUS"

By Lloyd O. Ivie

Not so long ago a young man said to me, "I am not religious." I exclaimed in my heart, but not to him, "You know not what you say, or I am sure you would never say that." Then I asked, "Do you know what religion means?"

There are various definitions in the minds of people, perhaps, as to just what religion means.

Yet, religion is life.

This means that religion is a vital power which touches every phase of human effort and activity. Morals, ethics, science—religion embraces them all. Religion is older than all.

Religion implies, "Thou shalt not lie," "Thou shalt not steal," "Thou shalt not kill," "Thou shalt not bear false witness," "Thou shalt not covet." It also demands, "Honor thy father and thy mother," and "Do unto others as ye would that they should do unto you."

Then, he who says, "I am not religious," would lie! He would also steal! He might even kill; and why should he not covet? What power could there be which would restrain him from dishonoring his father and mother?

As well might he say, "I am untrustworthy," "I will not tell you the truth," "I have no respect for my parents."

He who has said, "I am not religious," may be likened unto a chimney sweep, who after having spent his life in soot and smoke would exclaim, "I am not black." Or, he may be likened unto a miller who would say, "There is no flour upon me."

He who rejects religion is in rebellion against truth. He denies the power which created him. He spurns the very environment which has constructed civilization. He ignores the very tree upon which he has been born a leaf.

He tacitly testifies that he is ignorant and foolish, that he is stubborn and self-willed. He stands as a witness that he would rather have his own way than the right way. He has driven a poison sting into his own flesh.

In fact, he who says, "I am not religious," certainly does not comprehend what he says; or it would be the last thing on earth he would ever think of saying.

Lyman, Wyo.

For the New Year

May Truth and Love my course decide, throughout the year to come;
Truth, the beacon light of life, goal of the race well run,
The never changing prize to seek, whose fulness makes us one,
With God, the Eternal Father, and Jesus Christ, his Son.

May Truth and Love abide with me, throughout this glad new year;
Love, the spirit that was His, dispelling hate and fear,
That priceless, tender, touch of Him who dries the widow's tear.
Restraining greed, uplifting life, and bringing Heaven near.

Oh, Truth is life eternal, for back to God 'twill lead,
And Love a light from Heaven brings, the soul and heart to feed,
These two encompass all the rest; I'll need no other creed,
If I but learn to live them well, and to their voice give heed.

Los Angeles, California.   ERNEST W. BOSGIETER

IMPROVEMENT ERA, FEBRUARY, 1927.

Two Dollars per Annum

Entered at the Post Office, Salt Lake City, Utah, as second-class matter

Heber J. **Grant,**   }Editors   Melvin J. Ballard, Business Mg
Edward H. **Anderson.**   }   Moroni **Snow,** Assistant.

*Acceptance for mailing at special rate of postage provided for in Section 1103, Act c
October 3, 1917, authorized on July 2, 1918*

CONTENTS

Advertising Policy of the Era

We accept only the highest class of advertising. We recommend to our readers the firms and goods found in our advertising pages.

ADVERTISERS IN THIS ISSUE

HUMOROUS HINTS

Seasick—They were at sea—the sea was rough,
"You're not as sick as I," said she,
"No, but I feel so awful tough,
I'd hate even to yawn," said he.—*A. H.*

* * *

A Difference—Some lie beneath the starry sky,
And some there are who never lie.—*A. H.*

* * *

Height of Modesty—Then there's the girl who always carries a handkerchief cover her knees when she sits down.—*Perrins.*

* * *

As Understood—Stranger: "I represent a society for the suppression of pr fanity; I want to take profanity entirely out of your life, and—"
Jones: "Hey, Mother! Here's a man who wants to buy our car."—*The Furro*

Young Man Musician: "I'm glad you came to recital last night. During the
first part of the evening I felt that I was making a fool of myself."
Old Lady (intending to offer encouragement): "Everybody thinks the same."
—*D. C. R.*

* * *

The absent-minded man fell into the lake. His rescuers had a hard time to
get him out.
When they finally succeeded he thanked them and gasped: "A very close shave,
indeed; and the worst of it, gentlemen, I've just remembered that I can swim."—*L. F.*

* * *

Prohibition Officer: "What's your name?"
Drunk: "Gustavisis Ijbre Hoodligxz Carciytgr Intogefketen—"
Officer (putting book back into pocket): "Well, don't let it happen again."
—*L. F.*

TRAVEL AND

New Classes being formed every day
Enter Any Time

Why attend the L. D. S. Business
    College?

Best courses of study.

Best teachers, specially train-
    ed, experienced and successful

Best methods.

Best equipment.

Best returns for your time and money.

L. D. S. Business College

SALT LAKE CITY

"The School of BEST Results"

INDIVIDUAL SACRAMENT SETS

NOW IN STOCK

*Best in the
market*

*will last a
life time*

*—36 glasses in
each tray*

RECOMMENDED BY PATRONS. REFERENCES FURNISHED

Made especially for L. D. S. Churches, and successfully used in Utah
and Inter-Mountain region, also in all Missions in the United States, Europe, and Pacific Islands. Basic metal, Nickel Silver, heavily plated with
Solid Silver.

SIMPLE, SANITARY, DURABLE

Satisfaction guaranteed. Inquiries cheerfully answered.

ONE OF MANY ACKNOWLEDGMENTS

Bishop's Office, Bern, Idaho, May 2, 1921.

"I am in receipt of the Individual Sacrament Set, consisting of four
trays and the proper number of glasses.

"Everything arrived in good condition. We are very pleased with it.
I take this occasion to thank you for your kindness."

BUREAU OF INFORMATION

Temple Block   Salt Lake City

*WHEN WRITING TO ADVERTISERS, PLEASE MENTION THE IMPROVEMENT* B

"TO BECOME BETTER ACQUAINTED WITH
THE DOCTRINES AND IDEALS OF THE
CHURCH."

*CULTIVATE THE READING
HABIT NOW.*

Get all your Church Books from us.

Deseret Book Company

44 East on South Temple

That's what ETHYL GAS will do,
Make the Carbon work for you,

Turn the Carbon into power.

Get extra Mileage without "Knocks" with

BENNETT'S
ETHYL   [RED]   Gasoline